Be

and

Bachelors

Kathryn Brown

CJ Publishing

Published in 2013 by CJ Publishing

Copyright © Kathryn Brown 2013

ISBN: 978 - 1490900889

Typeset by ReallyLoveYourBook, Bridgend, UK

Printed by CreateSpace

Chapter One

A midweek drinking session with Alfie and Jez always resulted in a discombobulated brain and the awful realisation that I'd have to get myself into work under the pretence I was fully functioning. As a twenty-seven year old man with a relatively good job, living with my mum wasn't exactly where I wanted to be but unfortunately finances dictated otherwise. It wasn't a bad thing, living with mum; she did my washing and cooked my meals, but to have her shouting up the stairs, yelling at me to get my lazy arse out of bed was something I wouldn't have missed should I have had my own place. I guess you could say we looked after each other; she waited on me hand and foot whilst I kept her fit and active, and at fifty-one, I'm sure she was grateful.

Incredibly, my legs swung over the bed and my feet hit the floor with a thud, before the rest of me made an agonising lunge forward in the hope my head hadn't stayed where it was, nicely nestled on the pillow. Mum must have heard the thud but unfortunately it didn't deter her from barging into my bedroom. For a moment there was silence whilst she looked around the room, her eyes scanning every nook and cranny. It was when she thrust her hand to her mouth and gasped that I realised I was in for it. It was my sanctuary, my little corner of the house that she left untouched, though I often wondered if she ever had a rummage when I was at work. She'd never mentioned my collection of magazines under the mattress so I did wonder if she'd kept to her word about never going in my room when I wasn't in. But her dramatic heel-turn and determined march out the door confirmed that my mother most definitely had never entered my personal space. At least not recently.

"Bloody hell, son, what's that smell?" was all she could say as she quickly left the room, obviously horrified at the state of it. I trudged into the bathroom, my feet doing all the work, my head just following my footsteps. The tiled floor helped a little, bringing me round slightly from the fog my brain was having trouble shaking off. The bathroom was cold, as usual. I turned on the shower and waited for the water to warm up then stepped under it, a feeling of relief massaging me as the bursts from the shower head hit my skin like a million needles. Mum had done good going for a power shower after having the bathroom done up last year. We were sick of a trickle and desperate for a proper shower so she splashed out and had a double shower installed with a new power generator. She increased my rent a bit which I knew she would; being Scottish I suspected she wasn't going to let me get away with paying the same when I used the shower every day and we were on a water meter. But the fact it was a double cubicle excited me because at the time I was going out with Bethany Calder and she was a little on the large side, which was what split us up in the end after I got rat arsed one night and told her 'yes, your bum does look big in that, but your bum looks big in everything.' I realised afterwards that I was for the chop and tried to backtrack by telling her I much prefer a bit of meat on a woman and wouldn't have her any other way, but the hole I'd dug was too deep and she dumped me.

I did actually like Bethany even if she did have a fat arse, but she was kind and gentle and her mum made a neat lasagne every Friday night before we'd hit the town. Said it was to line our stomachs because she expected us to end up in A&E having them pumped by two-am judging by the state of us on a Saturday morning. Come to think of it, I probably fancied her mum more; a tall, slim woman with pert tits and a cute smile. I never met Bethany's dad as he ran off with their next door neighbour when she was eight and never bothered with Bethany after he left, but I reckon she was like him. Her mum was cool and trendy, always up for a laugh. She worked in the White Horse behind the bar and I still see her in there when I venture in on a Saturday night with the lads. We don't hang around for long though because Bethany often turns up with her new boyfriend, a six-foot-six body builder who's built like a brick shit house and works on the door at Tango's. The first time I saw her with him I thought she'd hired a hit man and I left, not wanting any trouble. These days, however, they stand at the bar chatting to Carol, Bethany's mum, and fortunately ignore me. I suppose they're a good match really with her being on the wide side and him being a big bastard, but I can't imagine him carrying her over the threshold if they ever got married unless they were to live in a house with reinforced door frames.

I turned the shower off and felt a bit better as I stepped out and reached for the towel. At least I felt fresher even if my head was still hanging off. I heard the front door slam which would have been mum leaving for work. She liked to be there early. Her shift didn't start until ten but she always worried that her bus wouldn't turn up or she'd end up sitting next to Doreen Casey from down the road who pestered her about Jean Grundy's dog shitting on the pavement near the bus stop. Neither my mum nor Doreen has ever had the guts to mention it to Jean because she'd scare the shit out of Freddy Krueger, never mind her dog. Mum can't be doing with gossip so she gets the earlier bus thus avoiding Doreen and a conversation about dog shit. She works at Morrisons and has recently applied to be a shop floor supervisor. Personally, I reckon my mum would be good at it. She's bossy, assertive and takes no crap from anyone so I'm hoping she'll get the promotion. It'll mean some extra money in the kitty which is always a good thing, especially since dad got made redundant.

Mum kicked him out two years ago after he'd lied to her about his job. He's an electrician by trade and was working at a factory that makes plugs and sockets and electrical accessories. But when they offered him a tidy package and gave him a decent reference, he snatched their hands off and probably thought he could look forward to a couple of weeks holiday in the bookies and maybe treat mum to a new pair of shoes with any left overs. But mum found his redundancy letter a week after he'd finished at the factory, still believing he was going out to work every morning at eight o'clock with his packed lunch. Unfortunately for dad, by the time he got back from 'work' that evening he came home to a few black bin bags and a set of step ladders on the doorstep, and mum standing with her arms folded and the sternest of stern looks on her face. In hindsight, I wished I'd recorded his face because it was priceless, even if I did feel a bit sorry for him at the time.

"You lying bastard," she said, eerily calm. "We've never kept secrets, Brian, but you've made me see you in a different light." That bit always makes me snigger with him being an electrician. "I don't want you near me or my son. You are not welcome in this house anymore."

Dad looked at the bin bags then dared to look mum in the eye. "What are you talking about, you daft woman?" Then he noticed the step ladders. "And where did you find them? I've been looking for them for months."

"What I'm talking about, Brian, is that I know about you being made redundant and getting a few thousand pounds paid into your bank account. I found this." She waved the letter in front of his face and his eyes quickly scanned it. "When were you going to tell me?"

I think dad was a bit embarrassed at that point. His male pride seemed to take over and he went to pick up one of the bin bags. "Come on, Christine, let me explain." He picked up the bag and tried to shuffle his way past mum. But she stood firm.

"You're not coming in. It's been a long time coming and I've been meaning to do this for a while now but I'm filing for divorce. Our marriage is a sham. The only good thing that's come out of it is Gary." I swear I heard dad snigger at that point. "I think we'll both be better off if you find somewhere else to live and we get on with our lives, apart."

"But love, you're being ridiculous. I'm sorry I didn't tell you about the redundancy, I was ashamed. Never thought the bastards'd make me redundant but it's my age you see. Men at my age don't stand a chance when redundancies are on the cards. They gave me a good reference and I've put word out for some work." Mum waved another piece of paper in front of him. I don't remember where she got that from but my mum's always been magic.

"I've read your reference, Brian. I'm sure you'll get another job eventually and I wish you luck. But you won't be coming back here and that's final. Now take your clutter and bugger off." I saw her kick the bin bags and they toppled over towards dad's feet. Fortunately, she'd tied them up otherwise I suspect Mrs. Dean from next door would have had a field day inspecting dad's smalls as they were strewn over the front garden.

"Christine... love... let's talk about this." I feared dad was going to start begging but mum turned her back and walked into the hall before closing the door, surprisingly gently. She ushered me into the front room.

"I'm sorry you had to hear that, son, but your father's an idiot and he's brought this on himself. I'm sure you'll still want to see him but it won't be in this house." I stood and looked at her. Being a couple of inches smaller than me you'd think I'd have been a bit intimidating but it was the other way round.

"I didn't know you and dad were having problems. Why didn't you say anything?" She shrugged and walked towards the kitchen. I knew better than to ask any more questions, especially after I noticed the tears in her eyes, so I switched the television on instead and watched Eggheads. As I glanced out of the window I saw dad struggling with the bin bags as he bundled them into his car. The step ladders went on the back seat. I found out a few days later that he moved in with his mate for a while until he found himself a flat. I did want to go and see him but I felt I should stay loyal to mum for at least a few weeks, until the dust had settled. I could tell mum appreciated that because she kept bringing me cans of beer home from work and didn't complain when I brought Lucy Tamworth home for a one-night stand.

I must stop thinking about Lucy; every time I do it sends a shiver down my spine as I think about that firm arse and the thong she was just about wearing. Mum found it the next day shoved behind my chest of drawers – that was obviously where it landed when I pulled it off and threw it. Lucy had to go home commando, though she didn't complain and I imagine it wasn't a new experience for her. Our one-night stand turned into a few sessions at Jez's place when his mum and dad went to Tenerife for a fortnight. But by the time they got back

Lucy decided I was only after one thing and she walked out of my life for good. I don't deny I only liked her because of her ability to please, but I wouldn't have said no to a long term relationship with her, though it probably would have killed me in the end. "What better way to go than die on the job," my granddad used to say. He was a randy old bugger and I still miss him, four years on. We had some cracking conversations about when he was a lad and I was always proud when mum said I took after him. He was quite a looker in his day too, and very popular with the ladies, as he used to tell me. I reckon he'd have approved of Lucy Tamworth though I'm not sure what he'd have made of Bethany. Come to think of it, knowing how he never minced his words, I doubt I'd have ever taken Bethany to meet him, and maybe not Lucy, come to that.

Head still spinning and the remnants of last night's pizza poking fun at me from the cardboard box, I stumbled over the clothes on the floor and opened my wardrobe. The navy trousers would have to do, and the beige shirt that mum ironed the other night. I stepped into boxer shorts, pulled on some socks then put the rest of my clothes on, feeling a bit faint as I stood and looked at my reflection in the pine framed mirror. The bags under my eyes reminded me of dad's black bin liners that mum had bundled his clothes into and even though I'd managed a quick shave in the shower, I still didn't pass for Justin Chatwin. I told myself I'd have to do, time was ticking on and I could feel a few rumbles in my stomach. A strong coffee from Starbucks and a chocolate chip muffin would keep me going till fag break at half-past ten. Though that was something else I needed to think about giving up. Cigarettes were costing me a fortune and a night out with the lads these days was eating well into my wages. Jez and Alfie both had good jobs as managers and earned a lot more than me, plus they lived on their own in bachelor pads next door to each other. I wished I could have afforded to buy one in the same block but my job as a careers advisor at the local college didn't pay enough and I was struggling to save up a deposit. Mum said if she ever won the lottery she'd buy the whole block of apartments for me and I'm sure she would, just to get rid of me.

I grabbed my car keys from the hall table and bolted out the door, narrowly avoiding the postman as he stomped towards me. "Stick 'em through the letter box, mate, cheers," I said, though I doubt he heard me as he had earphones stuck in his ears and seemed to be doing a dad-dance towards the front door. The car did its usual spluttering before it finally came to life and I set off for work.

Chapter Two

I was greeted with lots of 'hi's' and 'awright's' as I walked down the path towards the main entrance of the college. The students were a great bunch and I'd grown quite fond of some of them over the years. I'd been a careers advisor for six years after deciding I didn't want to follow in dad's footsteps and be a tradesman at Victors. He was good enough to put a word in for me to management and they put me on a training scheme for twelve months after I left university, but I knew it wasn't what I wanted to do and the money was crap anyway. My heart had always been in teaching of some sort, or working in a college environment, and when I saw a vacancy advertised at Dullsdale College I couldn't resist applying. Never thought I'd get the job, especially when I went for the interview and realised I was up against some tough competition. A lot of the other candidates seemed to be a lot older than me, people in their forties and fifties, probably with a lot more experience than I had, but the boss said they chose me because I was like a breath of fresh air and would be able to relate to young people better than someone of a 'certain age'. I thought he sounded a bit age-discriminatory at the time but I obviously didn't say anything and shook his hand when he offered me the post. Mum was thrilled for me and went out the next day to buy me a new suit. Dad was a bit quiet for a few days after I'd told him the news and eventually said he felt embarrassed because he'd gone to a lot of trouble to get me that job at Victors. I didn't have the heart to tell him I hated working there and that my immediate supervisor was a complete tosser. Dad was a bit old-school and would have thought I was being disrespectful but he got over it in the end when he noticed how happy I was to get up in the morning and go to work. It was a new experience for dad; he'd never seen me happy to go to work.

"Gary, can I have a word with you at break time please?" Lisa Hill collared me on my way to the office. "I need to speak to you about Colin Jones, he wants to quit college and do some temp work as he's finding his course 'boring'." She emphasised the word 'boring', rolling her eyes as though she'd heard it all before. "I think it'd be better if you spoke to him and explained how important an education is before he starts to think about getting a job."

I nodded and smiled, not sure whether Lisa had noticed the bags under my eyes and coffee I was precariously balancing on top of a box file. "Send him to my office at about twenty-to-eleven and I'll have a chat with him" There was no way I was missing my fag break at half-past ten. She tottered off in her high heels, clacking along the corridor and waggling her pert bottom. I noticed a few testosterone-filled students ogling as they walked past, looking back with a grin and no doubt a few thoughts racing through their heads. It seemed a life time since I was a student but I knew exactly what they were thinking, because I was thinking the same.

Fag break came and went and Colin Jones knocked on my office door. "Come in," I called, pushing a few pieces of paper around the desk to make myself look busy. "Sit down, Colin, just give me a second." I always said that to the students because it made them think that being a member of the workforce meant you were always busy. It often deterred them from wanting to drop out of college and get a job, knowing that work was something you did on a regular basis unlike being a student which was something done when you didn't have a hangover. I opened and closed the top drawer in my desk then put my pen back in its little pot, an embarrassing pink mesh thing that mum had bought me from WHSmith.

"I hear you're thinking of quitting college?"

Colin nodded and gave me a 'can't be arsed' shrug. I knew where he was coming from because I'd been there and given up on the first course I did when I was only seventeen. Mum had forced me to do it, saying it was for my own good and that all boys of my age should learn to type. I was the only boy in the class and soon became a laughing stock. A class consisting of twelve girls, most of them who fancied me, and a mature student in her fifties who wanted to keep up to date with modern technology. She was actually the only sane one in the class and I used to sit next to her most days. The problem was, I was hopeless at typing and just wanted to earn some money so I could save up and get myself a car. I had my eye on a nicely polished Astra that was for sale in Abbey's Autos but mum was adamant that I got a skill behind me before I turned into a boy-racer and got my licence suspended for speeding. She's never had much faith in me, though looking back I can see her point. I'd already bought some 'go-faster' stripes and hubcaps so I guess her worries were justified.

"Tell me what you don't like about college, Colin. Maybe there's something we can do to make it more interesting for you." I wasn't building my hopes up.

"Dunno really," he shrugged. "Think I need a job more than I need to come here."

"And what kind of job do you expect to get?"

"Dunno." I could see Colin hadn't really thought this through.

"Well, let's start from the beginning." He sighed and repositioned himself on the chair, realising he was here for the long haul. "The course you're on is..." I lifted a piece of paper. "Computer studies." I looked up at him and smiled. "That's a really useful course, Colin, one that will put you in good stead for the future. Everything's about computers these days you know." Now I was starting to sound like my dad.

"I can get round computers no problem," he replied. "I just find the course crap. It's the same thing over and over, and I already know most things." Cocky little bastard, I thought.

"So do you think you need a more stimulating course perhaps? Something to sink your teeth into?"

"Yeah, probably, I dunno." Thought we might have been getting somewhere for a moment as his eyes lit up when I said the word 'stimulating'.

"If you have technology and computer qualifications behind you, I guarantee you'll find a job when you leave here. And what about university? Have you thought about further education?"

Once more Colin shrugged. "Can't be arsed with uni. Who wants to be in debt up to their eyeballs before they've even started work? Nah, it's not for me."

"Okay, I can partly understand that but it is worth looking into, don't dismiss it just because of the debts. We all get into debt at some stage of our lives." I picked up the college prospectus and opened it to the page titled 'Courses in Technology'. "Let's have a look, see if there's a better course you could be doing, something a bit more, err, interesting."

Colin shuffled again on his chair and looked at the clock on the wall. "I just want to leave and find a job," he said.

I ignored him and showed him the page I'd found on alternative courses. "Look at this one; it's part time and a couple of evening sessions. Looks a lot more intense than the one you're currently doing. And then there are a couple of diploma courses. Why don't you take this book away and discuss your thoughts with your parents, I'm sure they'll be able to help you as well."

Colin laughed. "My parents? Are you kidding? They couldn't give a shit if I'm at college or in Timbuktu. I hardly ever see them except on a Sunday when dad's run out of beer money. Nah, I just want to sign the papers and leave."

I started to feel a bit sorry for him. Even though mum had forced me to do the typing course, at least it was because she cared about my future. I closed the book and passed it to Colin. "Have a look through it. There might even be something completely different you fancy, something that has nothing to do with computers. Don't just give up like that, mate, we can't go through life giving up at the first hurdle." I stood up, my cue to say the meeting was over and he was dismissed. I walked around the desk and put my hand on his shoulder. "I'm always here if you need to chat, and even if you do quit, you're still welcome to pop in and see me if you need any advice."

Shuffling out the door and leaving it wide open, I shook my head and thought about the future generation and how hard it was for them to find a job these days. It wasn't going to be easy for Colin, he had little confidence and his attitude left a lot to be desired. I let the fact that he hadn't said thanks for my advice wash over me and put it down to him being seventeen. But really, I'd been brought up to use my manners and couldn't help pity these kids who hadn't.

I went into the precinct at lunch time and sat in Jack's cafe munching on a cheese and pickle sandwich with a cup of strong tea. It was a place I frequented mainly because I fancied Janice who worked behind the counter. She was a tall, blonde woman with a soft complexion and just the right amount of makeup. Her eyes were blue and the bottom strands of her hair curled as they rested on her shoulders. She didn't wear a wedding ring and I wasn't sure if she had a boyfriend, though I intended to ask her out at some point, only I'd never had the guts. Billy Brown who also worked in the cafe seemed a bit too familiar with her and I'd often watched them flirting behind the caffettiere, fiddling about with milk jugs and giggling over the muffins. I didn't like him much, he reminded me of a bully at my old school. A guy called Jason Fleet who had just about shagged every bird in our year and moved on to their mothers. When me, Jez and Alfie were chatting to a group of girls one break time whilst having a fag in the bike sheds, Jason and a couple of others ganged up on us and told us to move on and leave the girls alone. Jez made the mistake of standing up to Jason who then swung a fist at him which landed on my right cheek. My mum went ballistic at the Head teacher the next day and Jason got suspended which meant my life at high school was destined to be hell forever.

He didn't disappoint. He hounded me for six months

after that incident, tormenting me with threats that he would throw a brick through our window and terrorise my mother. I ignored most of his threats mainly because he didn't know my mother who wasn't the sort of person to let a spotty fifteen year old kid terrorise her. But it did become a pain in the arse when he kept hiding my uniform during PE, and one day managed to put my shoes on the school roof. The caretaker had to climb up and rescue them, but unfortunately not before a flock of pigeons had shat all over them. I didn't tell mum what had happened and just cleaned them up myself. The last thing I wanted was for her to go marching into school again and for Jason Fleet to make my life an even bigger misery. I must admit it spoilt the last eight or so months at high school even though me, Jez and Alfie still had a laugh on the outside.

So there I was, finishing off the cheese and pickle sandwich when Janice came over and asked if I wanted more tea. She had a pot in her hand and I thought she'd come over specially, even though I didn't want another cup. I noticed Billy watching in the corner of my eye.

"Are you and Billy an item?" I haven't a clue where that came from. I sat for a moment and wondered if I was still drunk from last night. Janice smiled at me and shook her head.

"No, we're just mates. I've known him for years. What makes you ask that?" The way she spoke was like nectar soothing my senses.

"You always seem quite close. I just assumed you two were together."

"I couldn't go out with Billy, he's more like a brother to me."

"Well in that case, would you let me take you out sometime?" There I was again, words falling out of my mouth like I wasn't bothered about making an idiot of myself.

She smiled and tilted her head. "Aww, that's really

nice of you. I'd love to go out with you sometime."

I took a swig of tea. "Great. I'll pop back in tomorrow and we could arrange something maybe."

"I don't work on Saturdays. I'll be back in on Monday morning."

"Oh, right, well, how about I pop in for lunch on Monday and we can sort it out then?"

"Yeah, sounds good." And with that, she turned and went back to the counter and a very anxious looking Billy Brown. I saw him mumble something to her and she threw her head back and whispered in his ear, then she turned around to look at me again and smiled that infectious smile.

That afternoon at work went quickly and by the time I had chance to look at the clock, it was already gone four. I saw students making a hasty exit, a few standing around the car park admiring each other's Clios and no doubt pretending the BMWs they'd driven were theirs and not their dad's. I chuckled when I saw them because they reminded me of myself. Sometimes, during my student days, dad used to let me take his Audi to college, albeit a clapped out one, but it was still a car, and it would turn heads when I screeched into the car park, windows down, music full blast. It didn't impress the staff of course but the girls in my typing class thought I was well cool. Those were the days I enjoyed and I'd often take a few of them for a spin at lunch time, showing off as we drove through McDonalds.

I took Karen Harpinger out in it one night to the pictures. I was eighteen and a man on a mission, mainly a mission to get in her knickers but I didn't tell her that of course. I'd fancied her since the first day and was determined to do something to impress her. When she saw me roll up in dad's Audi that first time I borrowed it I knew I'd got her attention. The film we saw was a bit shit but the events that happened afterwards were a turning point for me and one that taught me a very valuable lesson.

I took Karen to a remote part of land overlooking the town of Bedworth. I turned the engine off and leant over for a kiss but she turned her head.

"What's up?" I asked, a bit surprised at her reaction. I mean, she must have known what I wanted when we drove six miles out of our way to a well-known sandy-textured bit of waste land otherwise known as 'dogger's beach'.

"I think you only want to shag me. I thought you wanted to take me on a date but now that you've brought me here I've realised you just want your leg over." She had it in one.

"Aww, come on, Karen," I pleaded, hoping she wasn't going to ask me to take her home. "I thought this was what you wanted?"

"I don't know," she dithered. "I haven't been brought up to come to places like this. My mum warned me about boys who only want one thing."

"I don't want one thing, Karen, honest." I was good at lying back then. "I really like you." Apart from which I'd just spent a tenner at the pictures and treated us both to a McDonalds.

"So have you brought me here to talk?" She had a point.

"Well, err, shall we get in the back, it's probably more comfy." Shit, I'd been too forward.

She looked around then seemed to gaze at my crotch area. "Yeah, go on then," she replied, much to my surprise. So we got out of the car and into the back where it really wasn't comfy at all but at least we could have a snog without getting prodded by the gear stick.

I leant over to her and put my arms around her. She

responded by kissing me hard on the lips. I never realised how strong she was until she forced me over on the seat and straddled me. I felt my life was in her hands for a moment and no matter how hard I tried to get aroused, it just wasn't happening. The bottom line was, she didn't turn me on and I was embarrassed about her sudden strength, not to mention the fact one minute she was more or less calling me a pervert and the next she was ripping my clothes off. Having always been a gentleman, I preferred a bit of kissing to get me in the mood first, and a good feel of what lay beneath the clothes.

"Get 'em off, Gary," she said, tugging at my jeans. "Here." She unzipped her cardi, revealing just a bra underneath (I hadn't seen that coming) and thrust her tit in my face. I didn't know whether to choke or give it a good squeeze but by the time I clasped my mouth around it I could feel her rubbing her hand against my cock, no doubt feeling quite annoyed that it wasn't standing to attention. "You alright?" she asked. "Aren't I turning you on?"

At that point I pushed her off me and sat up, discreetly feeling myself to make sure everything was intact. She sat and stared at me, gobsmacked at my inability to satisfy her. Her tits were still bare after she'd pulled the bra cups down and I was struggling for where to look, knowing my line of vision was either going to be a couple of pert breasts that should most definitely have turned me on, or an angry face waiting for an explanation. I had nowhere to run and all I could think of was getting her home.

"I'm sorry, Karen, I think I'm just cold, probably coming down with something. I wasn't feeling too great this morning." I did a dramatic sniff. "Maybe it'd be best if I got you home and we did this another time?" Like in another life perhaps.

"Well that's just charming that is. You bastard." She

had a way with words did Karen. "You've brought me up here for a shag and expected to have to talk me into it, thinking I was frigid and I'd be an achievement for you, something you could brag to your mates about. 'That frigid little virgin who never lets anyone get in her knickers was mad for me.'" She emphasised that last sentence to make me feel bad. "Well I'm not frigid and I'm not a virgin and for your information I've been here loads of times. You're full of yourself you are, full of bullshit and testosterone. 'Gary Stringer, the gay boy who couldn't get a hard on even with a tit in his gob'." She emphasised that bit, too. I was starting to feel a bit worried about Karen's intentions and my thoughts began drifting to the school bully, Jason Fleet. I had an awful feeling about this.

"Let me take you home, Karen. I'm really sorry." I tried to talk her round as we got back into the front seats and fastened our seat belts but she carried on goading me and making me feel like a complete loser.

"You wait till I tell the others tomorrow. You'll never live this down. Gary pencil-dick Stringer who couldn't get it up."

"Yeah, alright Karen, you've made your point. I've apologised."

"You're a big show off, taking me out in your dad's Audi and thinking you're god's gift. You're pathetic."

"And you're an ungrateful cow," I mumbled.

"What did you say?"

I pulled off 'dogger's beach' and onto the main road, putting my foot down, eager to get Karen home to save my ears from anymore insults.

"I said you're ungrateful. I've taken you out and spent a fortune on you tonight, Karen. And you've treated me like shit." I was getting going now. "I don't think you're frigid and I couldn't care less if you're a virgin or not but I think we both wanted the same. You didn't complain when I turned on to 'dogger's beach'." I had her there.

"Of course I didn't complain because I haven't had a shag in ages and I thought I'd play hard to get for a while, until you started lying to me about not wanting one thing." There were no flies on Karen. "I thought maybe the fact you'd taken me to McDonalds and the pictures might mean you really did fancy me after all but Sharon Grundy warned me yesterday when I told her we were going out tonight, she said you were a horny bastard and probably only wanted to dip your wick." Girls today, I thought, so unladylike.

"I'm sorry I lied to you..." I thought I should come clean as it didn't really make any difference anymore, "...but if you must know, I did fancy you, that's why I asked you out. I've always fancied you but never had the guts to ask you before. If you want to start spreading rumours about me around the college then go ahead. It won't matter anyway because I'm leaving soon."

"You're leaving?"

"Yeah, had enough of sitting in a class with a bunch of giggling girls and a woman old enough to be my mother, talking to me like I'm as thick as pig shit. I never wanted to do that stupid course in the first place but my mum forced me. So you'll be shot of me soon and you won't ever need to see me again."

There was silence for a few minutes. It was quite pleasant actually. I could see Karen's street come into view and I indicated, hoping she wouldn't say anything else before getting out of the car. No such luck.

"So you're a mummy's boy as well then? God, you're pathetic. I'm glad I found out what a loser you are before I let you shag me in your dad's car." And with that parting shot she got out and slammed the door, making the car shudder.

I screeched off and raced home, worried sick about going into college the next day and the possibility of facing Karen's wrath, not to mention a dozen sniggering college kids and no doubt many more when their mates found out about my 'pencil-dick'. I arrived home in a puff of smoke to see my dad looking out the lounge window. He got to the front door in record speed because he was standing on the step by the time I switched the engine off.

"Had a good night, son?" he asked. I shrugged and gave him the car keys. "Where did you end up?"

"Just took a girl from college to McDonalds and the pictures. Don't think I'll be seeing her again though." Thought I'd keep my cool; my dad was always impressed when I stayed focused when discussing girls.

"Hope there was no nonsense in the back of my car, son?"

I tutted and stormed into the house, rushed up the stairs and slammed my bedroom door. I wasn't in the mood for a conversation about my night out. In fact, I didn't want to think about it ever again. Unfortunately, Karen had other ideas as I learned the next day when I arrived in college to a very quiet classroom, filled with twelve smirking faces and a 50-something woman unable to look me in the eyes. I realised then that I couldn't stay on that course and by break time I'd signed the papers and quit.

Chapter Three

*T*he weekend went by in a haze of hangover and listening to mum sing along to Barry Manilow. I stayed in my room most of Saturday thinking of somewhere nice I could take Janice. I wanted to make it a special night, one she would tell all her friends about...one they'd all gasp at and be impressed by. Looking through the phone book at Restaurants I found the number for a posh Italian in Bedworth called Luciano's. I'd never been but mum and dad had eaten there a few times, mainly special occasions as my dad always pointed out, due to it being expensive. I decided to pop into town later that day and pick up a menu to get an idea of their prices. I didn't want to go out of my way to impress Janice then find out I couldn't afford to pay the bill. My credit card had taken a right hammering recently after I'd had work done on the car and I couldn't possibly ask mum for a loan again. The last time I asked her she told me I should get in touch with dad and start asking him for money but the last time I'd asked him for money, he'd told me to ask mum. At 27 years old with a decent job I should've been able to afford to take Janice to any restaurant I wanted and not have to worry about paying the bill but all this saving up I was doing was taking its toll. I'd been dipping into my savings for a while now and it was quickly diminishing. I'd be in my late 30's before I could afford to move out of mum's and then it would only be a studio flat, not flash enough to entertain the ladies in. I really envied Jez and Alfie and they'd offered for me to go and live with them on many occasions, but getting my washing done and meals cooked for me by mum was just too much to give up.

"You going out tonight, son?" my mum asked as I clattered down the stairs with the phone book.

"Popping to Alfie's, it's his birthday next week so we're having a few bevies at his place. Don't wait up as I might stay over."

"I never wait up for you, love. I need my beauty sleep." I actually thought my mum was attractive for her age and I went to give her a little peck on her cheek. "Ooh, what was that for?" she asked.

"Because I love you."

"You got a girlfriend at long last?"

"Might have," I grinned, before putting the phone book back in the cupboard and leaving the house.

As I thought, the prices at the restaurant were out of my league and I wondered if taking Janice there would be a mistake. I didn't know her that well, only from working in Jack's cafe, but I got the impression she wouldn't have been too chuffed with a suspicious horse burger and fries from the local burger joint. Plus, she always came across as someone with a bit of class, not like my other girlfriends, and so I decided to throw caution to the wind and offer to take her to Luciano's in the week. When I got home mum had left a twenty pound note on the telephone table with a note,

"Get some beers for Alfie and wish him a happy

birthday from me. Have a good night. Love you xx"

My mum was the best. I quickly showered and shaved and chose a pair of jeans and a shirt to wear before leaving the house with mum's twenty quid and my house keys. I stopped off at the off licence and got a few cans, putting the change in my pocket, knowing mum wouldn't bother that I'd only spent a fiver of her money. If I was to give Janice a night to remember I needed every penny I could get my hands on.

Jez was already sat on Alfie's sofa when I arrived, a can of Fosters in his hand and the TV remote in the other.

"Awright, mate," Jez shouted as I walked through the hallway to join him. Alfie was in the kitchen rustling up a curry. I put the cans on the coffee table and plonked myself into the armchair.

"What's been happening?" I asked, as Alfie came through and offered me a beer.

"Just the usual. Work and no play, you know the score." Alfie sat on the sofa next to Jez. "I've invited a few neighbours round, hope you don't mind?"

"Which neighbours," I asked.

Alfie looked a bit shifty. "Cath from down the hall, Julie from the first floor and Izzy from over the road. They hang out together at weekends and I saw them earlier coming back from town." He took a swig of lager. "I asked what they were up to tonight and they said now't, so I offered for them to come in for a drink." I was racking my brain trying to think of who Alfie meant. None of the names rang a bell and I wondered for a moment if he'd made them up and was really just trying to set me up with a one-night stand from the 'drop-ya-knickers-for-a-tenner' district, a small area of Bedworth that was well known for prostitution.

"How well do you know these girls?" I asked.

Alfie looked at Jez and they started grinning and shaking their heads. "Chill out, man, they're decent enough. Nice looking birds, all three of 'em. I've had my eye on Cath for a bit now and I reckon Izzy won't be backward in coming forward, eh Jez?" He winked at Jez as though he knew something I didn't. Jez laughed and gulped his drink.

"She's always up for it that one," he said, between burps and sofa shuffling. "I'm having her so that leaves you with Julie, Gaz. She's a nice girl, got a fit arse on her as well. You won't go wrong there, mate."

I wasn't too sure about Jez and Alfie's recommendations where women were concerned. They'd tried setting me up a few times in the past. One in particular was Jessie, a cute nineteen year old who'd been messed about by her boyfriend for a couple of years then had decided to ditch him and be on her own till she found Mr Right. I took her out for a drink one night, Jez's suggestion, then took her home and slept with her, Alfie's suggestion. Two months later, after I'd seen neither hide nor hair of her, she rang me up to tell me she was pregnant. When I finally came round and mum was leaning over me asking who was on the phone, I raced around to Jez's flat and told him what had happened. He was horrified and said he felt really bad for introducing us. It wasn't his fault of course but even though I'd had a lot to drink that fateful night, I was absolutely sure I'd used protection.

"Will you come with me when I go to see her?" I'd asked, causing Jez to fall over in hysterics at my cowardice.

"Fuck off, you knob," was his reaction.

I ended up going to Jessie's house later that day to talk to her and sort out what was happening, though I'm not proud to admit now that I was already visualising myself drawing money out of the bank for her to use at a private clinic. She opened the front door and when she saw me standing there, she took a step back as though she was in shock.

"Can I come in?" I asked.

"Well, err, not really. I've got me mate here. It's not convenient, like."

"Tell your mate to bugger off, we need to talk about you being pregnant."

She stood against the door, not budging, turning her head like the exorcist as though she was scared stiff of anyone coming into the hallway.

"Look Gary, can we talk another time. I shouldn't have phoned you out of the blue like that. I'm sorry. Maybe I could come to your house in the week?"

"But we need to sort this out now, Jessie." I raised my voice a notch. "You can't tell me you're pregnant then not expect me to want to talk to you." Just at that moment a tall, broad guy came out of a side door and into the hall, making his way towards us.

"Who's this?" he said, a bit too bluntly for my liking.

"Paul, this is, err, Gary, he's a friend from, err, college."

I looked up at Paul. He was a big bugger and reminded me a bit of Bethany's new boyfriend. I didn't want any trouble so I backed away. "Okay, I'll call you in the week and we can discuss it then." I started walking down the drive towards my car.

"Who the fuck's Gary?" said an angry voice behind me. I turned to see the big bugger standing over Jessie, looking a bit intimidating and not at all friendly. Against my better judgement, my defences kicked in and I turned to walk back towards Jessie's front door.

"Just go, will you," she said, "I shouldn't have rung you, just ignore what I said." I could tell Jessie was a bit frightened as her voice quivered.

"I'm not going anywhere. You're pregnant with my kid and I'm not leaving you alone with this angry bastard."

The angry bastard stared down at Jessie. "Pregnant with his kid?" he said.

"Aw shit, Paul, I didn't know what to do. You said you didn't want to be with me anymore and when I realised I was preggers I didn't know what to do, like."

"So you shagged that little tosser?" The angry bastard was really angry now and I took that as my cue to get away as fast as possible. It was obvious that he was Jessie's boyfriend and I'd guessed by then that the baby she was carrying wasn't mine at all.

I just reached my car in time before Paul thundered down the drive, shaking his fist and shouting obscenities that were no doubt making a few curtains twitch. It was like a scene out of Jeremy Kyle as I turned the engine and screeched off at what felt like a hundred miles an hour.

When I got home, fortunately in one piece, I rang Jez and told him what had happened and his advice was to lie low for a while, at least till Paul had calmed down. My lying low for a while turned into me not leaving the house for two months except to go to work, in case I bumped into the crazy son of a bitch. Jessie even had the audacity to ring me a few weeks later and apologise for involving me, saying the baby was definitely Paul's but she'd wished it had been mine because I seemed much more together and a better prospect than Paul who'd been inside four times and already had five kids with different women. After that, I never listened to Jez or Alfie on their recommendations of women. I considered myself to have had a very lucky escape.

It was gone ten when the girls arrived, a little tapping alerting us to them standing at the front door. Alfie went to answer it whilst Jez and I stayed seated, full of curry and verging on pissed. I must admit, when I saw Julie my first thought was 'get your gnashers round this'. Maybe it was the drink talking but she was definitely a bit of alright. Long brown hair, straightened and a bit jagged at the edges, really slim waist and a cleavage just poking out from the black top she wore. I wasn't going to get too excited but I was quite impressed that the guys had left me with the nicest looking of the three, in my opinion at any rate. Cath had huge tits so I could see why Alfie fancied her. He'd always been a breast man, anything with big jugs turned him on, whilst Jez was more refined. He liked his women curvy but not huge, tall but not over six foot and confident though not cocky. He was a picky bugger at the best of times but I guess that was why he was good at his job. Being the manager of a five star hotel meant he had to have pedantic tendencies to accommodate the clients who drove him nuts on many occasions with their whinging about toilet paper and room service.

I stood up and walked towards the girls who looked quite relaxed as they saw us. Alfie opened a bottle of white wine and poured three glasses, handing each one to the girls, then he passed a can to me and Jez, taking one for himself. "Sit down," he beckoned to the girls. I went to sit next to Julie on the sofa thinking we could get chatting but then Izzy plonked herself down in the middle of us. Very easy on the eye but a bit too confident for me. Jez kept looking over at her, probably weighing her up for later, but he didn't move and just carried on drinking his beer.

"How come you've got nowhere to go tonight then?" I asked, trying to break the ice or at least get Jez off his arse and start talking to Izzy so that I could get to know Julie.

"We have," Izzy said, a soft purr floating into my ear. "We're here."

The guys laughed, probably at my crap line of questioning but nonetheless it did break the ice and Jez finally got up and sat on the floor by Izzy's feet. Izzy stood up and Julie moved along, pushing her body against mine, then Izzy sat herself down on the floor next to Jez, and Alfie fell into a conversation with Cath on the sofa opposite.

It all seemed to be going well for a while. Julie told me about her job as an airline stewardess, making it sound ten times more interesting than mine, and Jez kept stroking Izzy's leg as though she were his pet spaniel. Alfie had put music on in the background, a bit of Adele to soften the mood. When I noticed the empty bottle on the table I asked him if he'd got another but he shook his head.

"No, mate, that's the only one I had."

I looked at Julie. "Do you fancy a walk to the shop to get another bottle?"

She hesitated for a moment then answered, "Yeah, all right. I'll buy it though." I wasn't going to argue so we stood up and got our coats on, leaving the others to enjoy Adele's dulcet tones.

When we got out of the building the cold air hit us like an arctic blast. "Cor blimey, it's cold innit?" Julie said, snuggling into me. I let my arm fall loosely around her shoulder.

"Clear sky, temperature's dropped. Do you want to go back in and I'll go to the shop myself?"

She shook her head. "No, I'd like a walk. Didn't really want to stay in that flat to be honest. I think Cath and Alfie are getting on really well and I wanted to leave them alone."

"What about Izzy, does she like Jez?"

"Oh yes, but she's a goer, always has been." I'd got that impression when she'd made herself comfy in between me and Julie at the beginning of the night.

"So do you have a boyfriend, Julie?" Thought I'd better get the unpleasantries out of the way before another brick-shit-house threatened to string me up.

"No, not anymore. I dumped him a few weeks back.

You might know him actually." I hoped I wouldn't. Or at least I hoped he wouldn't know me. "Colin Jones. He's a few years younger than me but he's such a loser. Thought he was mature and all, especially when he started a really good course at Dullsdale College. He has the makings of being a brilliant computer technician because he's really clever with stuff like that, but when we were together he kept saying he wanted to drop out." I was a bit stuck for words and just gawped at the pavement. At least Colin wasn't a brick-shit-house. "I felt sorry for him at first, thinking he just needed someone to encourage him because his mum and dad are pretty useless. But he was adamant about getting a job and he's got his heart set on working at Abbey's Autos, training to be a mechanic. His heart's in cars you see, not really computers. Anyway, I tried to encourage him to at least stay and finish the first year but he said he couldn't be arsed. I don't know what happened because I decided we weren't right for each other and I finished with him."

I wanted to tell Julie that Colin had indeed dropped out of college but obviously I couldn't say anything. I'd never broken confidentiality and wasn't going to start now. We approached the off licence and went inside. A bored looking man was sat behind the counter watching a cowboy film on the television, just about managing to look up when he saw us. Julie picked up a couple of bottles of white wine and took them to the counter, giving him a ten pound note and waiting for the change. The television continued to blare out and I don't remember the man saying anything to Julie as he gave her the change, all two pence of it.

I took the bottles from her, being the gentleman that I like to think I am, and then held the door open for her. She linked her arm through mine on the way back to Alfie's flat and we seemed to walk in sync. But all the while at the back of my mind, I couldn't help thinking of

Janice and the fact I really liked her. I knew spending a night with Julie could put a stop to any kind of relationship with Janice, she was too nice to be used. But I was growing to like Julie also and a part of me did want to spend the night with her, albeit in Alfie's spare bed, probably with the sound of him and Cath, Jez and Izzy humping in the next room. We'd had nights in like that before where a few girls had come round for drinks and a bite to eat. The walls were paper thin in the apartments and as I'm not the quietest person when I'm shagging the pants off somebody, I was a bit alarmed when I could also hear Jez moaning and his one-night-stand screaming "push it right in." Not the most relaxing way to spend a romantic evening, listening to your best mates filling their boots.

We arrived back at the flat and let ourselves in. Julie went straight into the kitchen and put the bottles of wine on the work top, unscrewing one and pouring it into a fresh wine glass. I went into the lounge. The sight that greeted me will leave me scarred for life. Cath was leaning over the sofa with Alfie poised over her, moving in and out against her backside as she turned to face me, her face screwed up and blotchy red, a moaning sound emitting from her lips as Alfie continued his quest for satisfaction. He didn't even look at me and just carried on humping Cath doggie-style against his cream sofa. Jez meanwhile, was lying on top of Izzy on the other side of the room, moving up and down frantically. Her legs were akimbo and "do it, do it, DO IT!" emanated from her wide open mouth.

I didn't know where to look so I made a hasty retreat for the kitchen, blocking the doorway so that Julie wouldn't walk in on the orgy that was taking place in Alfie's sitting room.

"What's up?" she asked.

"You don't want to go in there, not just yet anyway," I replied, still traumatised by the image of Alfie's arse.

"Why, what are they doing?" Was this girl a bit naive?

"They're, err, you know."

"What, shagging?" I looked at her, a slight embarrassment no doubt glazing over my eyes.

"Well, err, yeah."

"Well come on then, let's join in," she said, pushing past me with a glass of wine in her hand. I stared after her and watched as she confidently sauntered into the room. Wondering what the hell to do I breezed in after her, averting my eyes from Alfie's arse and closing my ears to Izzy's demanding pleas.

It was then that I knew I could never fancy Julie, not in a million years. Now don't get me wrong, I've never been frigid and I've always been up for a shag and have had more one-night-stands that I could fit on my bedpost, but when Julie starting stripping off and threw her knickers at me, I decided enough was enough. I wasn't about to have sex with her in front of the others, that just wasn't my style. And I was quite shocked that Alfie and Jez didn't seem bothered about the prospect. I threw Julies knickers onto the floor and left the room, going straight to the fridge for another can of Fosters. She must have grabbed her knickers quick because she pottered after me, dressed only in her underwear and high heels, looking every bit glamorous but just a little bit crazy. She wasn't my type at all.

"I'm sorry, Julie, I can't do that."

"Why not? What's wrong with group shagging? It's only an orgy, come on you boring fart. You don't need to touch the guys, just give us girls a good time. What d'you think we came here for when Alfie mentioned you and Jez were coming over for the night?"

I swigged the beer as though it was the last can on earth and I was determined no one else could have it. "I don't do orgies, never have and never will. If you want to join in go ahead, but don't expect me to."

"You're no fun." She sidled up to me and pushed her breasts against me, her hand reaching down for my cock, obviously in the hope of bringing it to life. But it wasn't going to happen. It was like being stuck in the nightmare with Karen Harpinger again and the memories of that night in my dad's Audi came flooding back.

I pushed Julie away and walked towards the door. "No, sorry Julie, I just can't do that. You go and enjoy yourself, I'm sure the guys will be glad to have another girl in there with them."

"Oh well, if you're sure, I mean I don't want you to feel forced into doing something you're not comfortable with."

A thought suddenly struck me. "Have you done this before?"

"What, threesomes and orgies? Oh yeah, loads of times."

"And do Alfie and Jez know you have?"

"Course they do. For fuck's sake, why d'you think they asked us here tonight. They wanted to give you a good time, said you'd been on your own for too long and needed a good seeing to."

"And where do you live, Julie?" My guts were doing somersaults now as it was dawning on me that I'd been lied to about the three girls who were supposedly Alfie and Jez's neighbours.

"We're not prossies, if that's what you're thinking. Well, I'm not. Cath's been in the trade and I know Izzy did a stint, but I've never worked for the industry. Never will either. I'm too choosy."

Bastards, I thought. Utter bastards had set me up. I fished about for my mobile phone and rang for a taxi. I couldn't believe my best mates had set me up like this. Something had told me when they'd first arrived that they were here for more than just a bottle of wine and a friendly chat.

"I'll see you, Julie." I opened the front door, a part of me feeling a bit disappointed that she wasn't who I thought she was. "Enjoy the rest of your night." She smiled at me and shook her head, probably thinking what a wuss I was, before she casually walked back to the lounge to join in with the orgy that was now at full volume and I suspect was reaching its climax.

Suffice to say I spent Sunday in a state of shock, not only with the image imprinted on my brain of Alfie's arse moving up and down against Cath, but at the fact my mates had thought it funny to set me up with a woman they hardly knew, throwing the three of us together to have an orgy in Alfie's sitting room. I thought they knew me better than that and I mulled over it all for a long time, thinking about the years I'd known both Alfie and Jez and wondering if I'd ever given them the impression I was literally up for anything. They knew me as a 'jack-the-lad', a fly-by-night that liked to impress the ladies and add as many notches onto my bedpost as I could before I found someone to finally settle down with, but this was something else entirely.

Mum kept knocking on my bedroom door trying to entice me downstairs with the smell of bacon and eggs wafting through the house. She left a tray outside my door at one point with a cup of tea and a few pieces of toast that miraculously she hadn't burnt. I sneaked out when I was sure she'd gone downstairs and grabbed the tray then dived back into my bedroom, scoffed the toast and switched on my mobile phone to a mountain of text messages from Alfie and Jez apologising and saying they thought I'd be straight in there. It was six o'clock when I emerged from my hovel and went to join mum in the front room, mobile phone at the ready as I'd finally decided ignoring my best mates wasn't the coolest thing to do.

"You all right, love?" mum asked, forever worried about me. Karen Harpinger hadn't been wrong when she'd accused me of being a mummy's boy.

I sat down next to her and nodded, staring at my mobile.

"Another hangover?"

"No, I didn't drink that much."

"You were in early. I didn't expect you home until this afternoon."

"Yeah, it wasn't that exciting really. Just me and the guys sat watching telly."

"Did you eat?"

"Alfie made a curry. It was good actually, he's quite a dab hand in the kitchen." That pleased mum.

"Do you fancy a Chinese for tea?" she asked, stroking my cheek like I was about 10.

I moved my head slightly. "Yeah, that sounds good. I'll go; I could do with some fresh air."

"Did you have any change from that twenty I gave you last night?" My mum didn't miss a trick.

"Only a couple of pounds," I lied.

"Oh well, I'll get another tenner and you can add the rest. Get me sweet and sour pork will you, and a portion of chips. And don't forget the prawn crackers." Mum opened her purse and pulled out a ten pound note, handed it to me and stroked my cheek again. "You look a bit peaky, love, are you sure you're all right?"

I stood up and put the money in my wallet. "I'm fine, honest mum. Just been really tired all day. Had a long week at work and think I might be ready for a holiday."

"A holiday?"She laughed. "You get more holidays than Jasmine Harman."

"Just because I get the same holidays as the students it doesn't mean I get a break like they do. I have tons of paperwork, and preparation. You know that."

"Well, I just don't like to see you looking so pale, son. Go and get some fresh air and stay off the booze tonight. You're drinking too much." My mum had an annoying habit of making me feel like an alcoholic. I left the house and walked down the street towards the Chinese chippy, wondering what I was going to say to Alfie and Jez when I texted them back later on.

The Chinese was empty and I was on my way back home within ten minutes, a bag full of delicious smelling food swinging from my left hand, my mobile in my right. A message came through just as I neared the house and I noticed it was from Jez.

"M8, me n A r worried bout u. Call soon."

I realised that letting them suffer for what they did to me last night had got a bit tiresome and so I decided to ring Jez.

"It's me."

"Fucking hell, Gaz, where've you been?"

"At home."

"Why didn't you ring us? We wondered where you were." I wondered why they hadn't been round if they were so worried about me. "We've realised we shouldn't have asked them tarts round last night and we're really sorry, mate. Didn't think you'd take it quite so bad. Alfie feels really shit about it."

"Forget it, man. Think it'd be better if we put it behind us and moved on."

"Yeah, that's the best thing, Gaz." There was a moment's silence. "But didn't you fancy that Julie bird? She was well up for it after you'd gone mate, you missed out there." I could tell he was grinning on the other end of the phone and apart from the fact my food was going cold, I really couldn't be arsed talking to him about Julie, who I'd actually thought was quite nice and maybe would have been 'up for it' one day with me and not the other two horny sods.

"Look, I'd better go as I'm standing on my door step

with a Chinese."

"Fit is she?" I heard hysterical laughter on the other end of the phone.

"Speak to you in the week, mate," and I hung up. I guessed it was pointless trying to tell Alfie and Jez how I didn't find group sex exciting, they'd have laughed at me and I doubt would never have understood. They might have had good jobs and a nice pad to live in, both driving around in flashy cars and always splashing their money about in the pub, but they really could be a pair of idiots at times.

Chapter Four

I couldn't wait for Monday lunch time to arrive and had sat watching the clock in my office for the past hour, wishing my life away. No one had knocked on the door and I could probably have got away with a crafty fag whilst hanging out the window, anything to calm my nerves. But the thought of seeing Janice was exciting me and I could feel a stir from time to time where there shouldn't have been one, especially not at work.

Finally, the clock struck midday and I picked up my keys and went into the hallway. Lisa Hill was swaggering towards me, her jugs sticking out and her nipples showing through her silk blouse. That woman could turn a monk on, I swear.

"Hi Gary," she purred. "Going out for lunch?"

"Yeah, just off to the precinct."

"If you fancy lunch with me sometime, you know where I am. I'm always on my own in the class room so just come and give me a knock, anytime."

"Sure, might just do that, Lisa," I said. The thought

of a choice between two very sexy women seemed quite exciting all of a sudden.

It was only a five minute walk to the precinct and Jack's cafe was a few yards through the main entrance. Janice was there, dressed in her uniform of white blouse, black trousers and white apron over the top. Her hair was tied back into a pony tail and it swished about her head as she turned around to serve someone. She noticed me as I walked in and smiled. It was a lovely warm smile that made me glow with pride. I knew there and then that I wanted to take her out and it had to be a classy joint like Luciano's. I went over to the counter, Billy staring at me again with thunder in his eyes.

"What can I get you today?" Janice asked, not taking her eyes off mine.

"I'll push the boat out and have a coronation chicken roll with a piece of millionaire shortbread." I nodded towards the coffee machine "And a coffee please, Janice. How are you?"

"All the better for seeing you," she replied, in a chirpy voice. "Go and sit down and I'll bring them over."

I made my way to the table and waited a few minutes before she danced towards me and gently put the tray in front of me.

"Do you still want to go out one night this week?" I asked, hoping I already knew the answer.

"Definitely. I get off work at five."

"Excellent. I can pick you up from home if you tell me where you live. I was going to book a table at..." I hesitated for a brief moment, "...Luciano's in Bedworth. Is that okay with you?"

"Wow. That's a gorgeous place. Are you sure? My mum likes going there but dad says it's too expensive to go on a whim." Result, she was impressed.

"It is a bit pricey, but I want to spoil you."

She laughed. "Make a good first impression more like." She knew me better than I thought.

"Well, if you like. Shall I book it then? Was thinking Wednesday?"

"Sounds fantastic. I can't wait to tell my mum."

"She doesn't want to come too does she?" I chuckled, hoping Janice would appreciate my little joke.

"She'd love to come. Shall I ask her?" Shit. I felt my stomach do a somersault and my whole body blush crimson red.

"Well, err, err..." Janice flicked her head back and laughed hysterically.

"Oh Gary, you're so funny. I was joking. Do you really think I'd let my mum come out with us? This is our first date and I hope it'll be one of many." She really was cute when she laughed.

"Phew," I said, lifting the coffee mug up to take a swig and stop myself from choking. "Sorry, guess I'm a bit naive sometimes. Write down your address and I'll pick you up at seven."

"I'll look forward to it. Here," she wrote her address down on a little notepad she'd pulled from her breast pocket, then ripped off the piece of paper and handed it to me. "I've put my phone number on there as well in case you get lost, but it's really easy to find."

I scanned over the address, noticing it was one of the better sides of town then folded it up and put it in my pocket. She chuckled again then turned on her heels and zigzagged her way through the tables back to the counter where Billy Brown was scowling so hard I thought he'd be able to lick his eyebrows.

<hr />

I tried to avoid Lisa Hill for the rest of the day as I'm sure the grin on my face would have been too obvious. But I also didn't want Lisa to think I was excited about her invitation to have lunch together. I was determined to give it a chance with Janice, after having my eye on her for so long. I knew that if things didn't work out there, Lisa would be waiting in the wings so at least I'd have someone to fall back on. Having gone without a girlfriend for far too long now I was getting a bit desperate to get back out there. I only hoped I didn't bump into Julie again though I knew it would probably happen with us both living in the same town.

Unfortunately, Lisa accosted me in the car park after work, almost forcing me against my car as she ran towards me.

"Gary, glad I caught you," she panted. "I wondered if you fancied a night out this weekend, say Saturday?" Under any other circumstances I would have said a resounding yes, but as I'd just arranged a date with Janice I didn't want to cock things up before they'd even got going. "What do you reckon, you up for it, Saturday night, a few pubs then back to my place?" Blimey, she wasn't shy.

"Yeah," I said. "That sounds great." Not sure if it was the 'back to my place' bit that made up my mind or the fact I'm a dick, but I couldn't resist those eyes and the nipples were back with a vengeance too.

"That's great," she said, smiling and inching a bit closer. "Maybe we could arrange where to meet up during the week, have lunch together perhaps."

"Okay, I'll come and find you later in the week and make arrangements." She stood and stared at me and for a moment I thought she was going to kiss me. I fumbled about in my coat pocket for my car keys, pulling them out and jangling them with enthusiasm hoping she'd register that I needed to go.

"Probably see you tomorrow then."

"Yeah, bye Lisa." I hit the button on the fob to unlock the car then opened the door. She slowly backed away, a rather disturbing grin appearing on her face as though to say 'You *will* see me tomorrow'.

As I drove home I wondered if I'd done the right thing in agreeing to go out with Lisa when I'd only just arranged a date with Janice. I'd known Lisa for four years and had watched her almost every day walk up and down the corridors at the college, jiggling her bum and thrusting her tits at anyone who got too close. I knew she'd had a long term relationship with Harry Lumber that I think lasted a couple of years, breaking down when he left and got a job at Newcastle University. They used to kiss and cuddle in the classroom and I walked in on them once, him with his hand up Lisa's blouse and her with her hand down his pants. I'm not sure who was more embarrassed, me or Peter Davies, a student whom I'd taken to see her.

"Shit, Gary, you could have knocked," Harry bellowed, and then saw Peter hovering behind me. He quickly fastened his zip and Lisa moved away from him, fumbling with the buttons on her blouse, red faced and flustered.

I only hoped Lisa wouldn't be expecting a fumble in the classroom as well as a cheese and pickle sandwich. I wasn't a saint by a long shot but I wasn't about to lose my job because of Lisa's lack of inhibitions. I didn't think it was a good idea to tell mum about Lisa so I filled her in on my date with Janice instead.

"Wednesday night, she's really nice, you'll like her."

"So do I get to meet her then?" mum asked, a sadistic look enveloping her expression.

"Maybe. Let me see how it goes first. I need to get to know her myself before I bring her here."

"Frightened I'll give her the inquisition?"

"Something like that." I grinned before going into the kitchen. "What's for tea?"

"There's a pizza in the fridge. I'm out with Claire tonight so you'll have to fend for yourself."

I did appreciate mum cooking for me and I didn't begrudge her nights out with Claire, her best mate. I took the pizza out of the fridge and grated some extra cheese on top then stuck it in the oven and sat at the kitchen table to read the paper.

"Where are you taking your new girlfriend?" Mum was stood at the door.

"She's not my new girlfriend yet." I didn't look up from the article I was reading, about some nutter who'd clipped a bus on the main road and turned his car over. "I'm taking her to Luciano's." I heard mum gasp.

"Wow, you don't do things by halves do you, son? It's expensive there. Can you afford it?"

I thought about that for a moment. "Well, so long as she doesn't want a bottle of their best champagne," I laughed. "I'll have to stick it on the credit card." I shrugged, hoping mum might take the hint.

"Do you really like this girl then?"

I looked up and noticed the serious expression on her face. "Yeah," I replied. "I've liked her for a while. I've wanted to ask her out for ages."

"And you think she'll appreciate somewhere like there?"

"Well she was dead chuffed when I told her that's where we're going. Why do you ask?"

"Your dad used to take me there when it first opened. I thought it was a bit posh really and overpriced but he liked it." For a moment I sensed she was going into a dream-like state, recollecting a date with dad from years ago, one that was obviously still fresh in her mind. "I'd like to lend you some money, son. You don't want to be clogging up that credit card. The interest payment on those things is ridiculous." I couldn't believe my luck. Mum went to her handbag and took out her purse. "Here," she said, handing me a couple of twenties and a ten. "Have a good time and make the most of it."

I took the money and looked at it. "You don't need to do that, mum," I said, like a fool. "But thank you, this will definitely help."

"You'll need it going there, son. It's not a cheap place. I only hope she doesn't expect you taking her places like that on every date or you'll end up in the gutter." Mum put her purse away and closed her handbag. "And if you get on okay, I want to meet her. It's been a long time since you brought a girl back here. I'm starting to wonder if you're gay."

I scoffed and closed the paper, having read the same paragraph five times. "Don't be daft, I'm not gay." My voice seemed to drop an octave. "I promise I'll bring Janice to meet you if it all goes well on Wednesday. You've probably seen her about town anyway. She works in Jack's cafe in the precinct near the college."

Mum looked deep in thought for a moment. "No, I don't think I know that place." She glanced at the oven. "That pizza should be done by now."

Chapter Five

I managed to avoid Lisa on Tuesday at work, narrowly escaping her as I made my way to the canteen at break time for a coffee. She was just leaving the staff room and I hid in the caretaker's broom cupboard. Apart from being whacked on the head by a mop and bucket, I managed to get to the first floor unscathed, where the canteen was situated, relieved that I didn't need to make arrangements for Saturday's date. After last night's conversation with mum about Janice, I imagined mum would be a bit pissed off with me if she thought I was up to my old tricks again.

"You can't two-time girls, it's just not right. You need to grow up." She'd said that at my twenty-first after she caught me snogging Phillipa Taylor in the cloakroom in the Brewer's Whistle Function Rooms. I was going out with Claire's daughter at the time (mum's friend). Helen was a lovely girl, though a bit boring. Jez and Alfie made a bet with me that I wouldn't get into Phillipa's knickers before I turned 21 and as I didn't officially turn 21 until 11pm, I thought I'd make damn sure I won the bet.

Unfortunately, mum opened her big gob and told Claire what I'd been up to and Claire subsequently told Helen who slapped me across my face before storming out of the function rooms in a huff. Claire shouted that she'd never forgive me for hurting her precious daughter but they got over it when they found Helen smoking pot the following weekend with Christopher Littlewood on 'dogger's beach'. I reckon her dad had been up there with someone but it was never confirmed, though I heard mum and Claire whispering in the kitchen one night not long after the pot-smoking event, and Claire sounded as though she was crying.

After that, I stayed single for a few months because Phillipa didn't want anything to do with me after she realised she was just a bet I won. I'd just started working at the college and was a cocky sod, but I soon got put in my place by Mrs Henderson who left soon after with a nervous breakdown. I remember Lisa telling me at the time she was on a slippery slope and the breakdown was imminent but my arrival hadn't helped plus the fact she considered me far too young to be advising scallywag students on career choices. Bit of an old-school tutor was Mrs Henderson and I did feel a bit sorry for her after she'd left, though I got her office so I didn't dwell on her nervous breakdown for too long.

"Gary," the voice shrilled in my ear, "can you stop a minute, I need to speak to you." It was Kevin Holloway, the college principal, someone I would rather not have stopped for when I was on my way to the canteen that was literally in sight. The fact I could smell bacon wafting down the corridor wasn't helping. "Sorry, I just need a word. Can you pop into my office before you leave today?"

I had no choice. "Sure, no problem." I noticed him hesitate. "Can I buy you a coffee?"

"Oh, not now, but thanks anyway. I've got a few meetings today and need to get on." He turned around and went towards the double doors that led to the staircase. I knew I'd spend the next few hours worrying about what Kevin wanted, he didn't usually ask for a word unless it was something serious. I'd never actually been summoned to his office before on my own, just with other members of staff for a quick team briefing, something I couldn't stand. They always amounted to nothing and none of the staff took any notice of what he said.

"Thanks for coming along to the briefing, guys," he always said, with an annoying chuckle at the end of his sentence as though he thought he was cool for addressing us as 'guys'. "I just want to touch base with you, see how the land lies, you know, make sure everything's tickety-boo." God, the man was an annoying twat. "Anyone got any issues they need to flag up?" Silence, every time. Then one day Clarissa Braithwaite piped up and nearly sent Kevin into an excited frenzy.

"One of my students has become very challenging and I think it needs to be discussed. I don't think this college is the right environment for him." It turned out the poor lad had just lost his mum and was in a state of grief and Clarissa couldn't cope with his rollercoaster of emotions, thinking he was disrupting the class and needed to be removed. As I knew Antony, the lad she was talking about, I decided it was my place to intervene.

"Antony is a very bright young man with an excellent future. Unfortunately, his mum has just died and he's obviously finding it very hard to come to terms with. I think some patience and understanding is required, Clarissa." She didn't like that, not one bit, and glared at me. I thought she was going to start crying for a moment and then I wondered if she was going to belt me one. But she turned to Kevin who was standing with his mouth wide open obviously wondering what the hell to say. As I'd only been working at the college a matter of months

49

and she'd been there for years, it did make her look like an idiot, but my little outburst made her hate me after that and she vowed never to have anything to do with me again. I'd often fantasised about her slim body and getting her into bed, but I had to come to terms with the fact that she would never be a notch on my bedpost.

The rest of the day seemed to drag and at four o'clock I made my way to Kevin's office. I knocked gently and waited for his response. "Come in," he bellowed. I opened the door and saw him sat behind his large desk in a plush leather executive chair.

"Gary, come on in and sit yourself down. Can I get you a coffee?"

"No thanks," I smiled, a bit bewildered by Kevin's sudden manners.

"I wanted to see you because I have an opportunity for you." I scanned the desk for my P45. "A vacancy has come up for Joe Mint's job, and I reckon you'd be just the right person." Joe Mint was Head of Communications, in other words, he did all the media work for the college and liaised with outside companies to get the students work experience and the possibility of a job at the end of their courses. It wasn't something I'd thought about doing because I quite enjoyed being hands-on with the students, talking them through their options and advising them on which careers best suited their abilities.

"Right, Kevin," I mumbled, racking my brain for something intelligent to say. "Well, err, thanks, I appreciate you considering me for the job." I shuffled about on the seat and crossed my legs. "Are there any other staff members who will be going for it?"

"Just a couple, but I'm confident that the job'll be yours if you apply. I'd put a good word in for you and between you and me," Kevin lowered his voice, "Joe reckons *you* should get it. He put your name forward."

Joe Mint was a nice enough guy, but I'd never really

had an intelligent conversation with him so I didn't really understand how he could have put my name forward. I'd had a laugh with him at a Christmas party one year when he got pissed and told me about his fling with a third-year student, something I'd been sworn to secrecy for, for obvious reasons, and I knew he was a bit of a rum bugger because I'd heard him often say how he'd like to shag Harriet Bell, the lady who worked in the front office. The fact he'd been supposedly happily married for years didn't seem to bother him. But I was now trying to fathom out how he could possibly assume I'd want to change my job from careers advisor to Head of Communications.

"When do you need my answer?" I asked Kevin, as he continued to try and read my expression.

"I'd like an answer in the next day or two, definitely by the end of this week. If I know that you want the job I'll just go ahead and get the forms filled in then I don't need to arse about advertising it. I'm sure a few will come forward but to be honest, I'm not sure, apart from you, that I'd want to give it to anyone else."

"Why is Joe leaving?"

"He's retiring. Wants to spend some time with his family he says. Though we all know the real reason, eh?"

I smiled, the emotion not quite reaching my eyes, and pretended I knew what he was talking about.

"Harriet, in the office?" Kevin said, rather smugly. "Her husband caught them last week." The smile reached my eyes.

"You're kidding?" I laughed, then realised how lame I sounded. "Gosh, I never would have thought." I was really digging a hole now.

"Everyone knew. I'm surprised you didn't." I think my face told Kevin more than I wanted it to. "It's best all round if he takes early retirement at the end of term, that way we won't be faced with any embarrassing scenes, if you get my drift."

I wasn't sure if the embarrassing scenes he referred to were Harriet's husband barging into the college to kill Joe Mint or Joe and Harriet being caught together by a staff member, or worse, a student. I nodded in agreement, remembering when I'd caught Lisa Hill in her classroom with her hand down Harry Lumber's pants.

"Anyway, that's all it was. If you could let me know one way or the other by Friday, I'd appreciate it." I took that as my cue to leave Kevin's office. "And Gary," I turned to face him, "not a word to any staff members, okay? Keep this between us for now, until we fill Joe's position. I don't want the others thinking I'm giving you preferential treatment."

"No worries, Kevin. And thanks again for considering me." I left the room, quietly closing the door behind me, and walked straight into Lisa Hill.

"Ooh, Gary, haven't seen you all day. Have you been avoiding me?"

I smiled at her, pretending I was pleased to see her. "Not at all, been a really hectic day, Lisa." I stifled a pretend yawn. "Better get off as I told mum I'd be home early tonight."

"What were you doing in Kevin's office?" she asked.

Trying not to call her a nosy cow, I smiled again and lied through my teeth. "A few issues that needed addressing, nothing important."

"You know you can always talk to me don't you, about anything?" She was standing extremely close to me now, my personal space completely invaded by her erect nipples. I can't say it felt unpleasant of course but I wasn't entirely comfortable. Then she ran her finger down my tie. "Anytime," she purred.

"Thanks, Lisa," I said, starting to back away. She was well up for it. "Sorry to be rude but I really do have to go."

"See you tomorrow. Have a nice evening."

"Yeah, you too." I quickened my pace towards the double doors and ran down the stairs two at a time, charging through the main entrance and almost kissing my car when I saw it reaching out to me in the car park.

I really did like Lisa but I was getting the impression she was a bit full on. I started imagining her as a bunny boiler, and if she found out I was taking Janice out the following night I was a bit worried about what she'd do. Her come-to-bed eyes and flirtatious actions definitely told me she liked me and that she'd most probably be expecting me to stay the night at her place on Saturday but I was starting to wonder if she had a cellar full of whips and creams and leather gear. Mind you, anything would have been better than the orgy at Alfie's the other night.

Talking of Alfie, I'd had a text message from him earlier on asking if he could come over for a beer. It was his birthday and I'd forgotten to send him a happy birthday message. I imagine he thought I was avoiding him after what happened, but it'd all been forgotten as far as I was concerned and I wanted to tell him about taking Janice out. I texted back that he could come over at eight and I'd provide the pizza and beer as a birthday treat. Then I added, 'and don't bring any girls'.

Alfie turned up at ten-past eight with Jez and some cans of beer. I let them in, noticing Jez winking at mum as he walked into the lounge. She'd put lipstick on for some reason and I reckon she'd brushed her hair as well. I only hoped Jez wasn't getting any ideas. My mum was out of bounds as far as my friends were concerned; she was my mum after all.

"I'll leave you boys to it," mum said, jumping off the chair and brushing past Jez, a little too frivolously.

"You don't need to leave on our account," Jez said.

"Mum's going out, aren't you mum?" I looked at her, willing her to grab her keys and coat and bugger off.

"I wasn't going to but I can always pop round to Claire's. But I won't be back late as I've got an early start tomorrow."

"We won't be staying late, Mrs Stringer."

Mum looked at Jez and rolled her eyes, making a camp hand movement. "Oh Jez, will you call me Christine? I feel so old when you call me Mrs Stringer. And besides, I'm not married anymore. I'm single now you know." I noticed her flutter her eyes at him when she said that.

"Bye, mum," I bellowed, urging her to leave the house. Thankfully she did. I turned to Jez. "Don't tell me you fancy my mother?"

"Your mum's hot, mate. I've always fancied her. Why, do you think I'm in with a chance?"

"No, you're fucking not," I snapped. "And don't get any ideas either. She's my mother for fuck's sake, well out of *your* league."

Jez laughed. "I'm sure your mum doesn't need your permission to go out with someone. I'm thinking of asking her to the races. She used to go with your dad didn't she?"

"I mean it, Jez. Leave her alone. I'll never live it down if you end up with my mother. And besides, you've shagged too many birds in this town and my mother won't be one of 'em." I cringed at that thought, wondering if my mum was still sexually active. Dad had been gone a couple of years and I didn't recall her having a boyfriend in all that time, though she had been on a few dates, one in particular with Derek Somersby from the supermarket where she worked. He'd come to the house to pick her up and took her into town for a meal. Come to think of it, I don't remember her getting home that night but I do remember the front door closing at about seven in the morning. I forgot to ask her about it as I was going through all the shit with Bethany at the time and everyone else's problems seemed much more trivial than mine.

"Get the pizza then, I'm starving here." Alfie's words brought me out of my trance, saving me from having flashbacks about Bethany's arse, and I went into the kitchen to slice up the pizza and grab a few cans.

I passed the cans round and put the pizza on the table, giving Alfie and Jez a plate each. "Cheers, Alfie. Happy birthday, mate," I said, as I hit his can with mine.

"Yeah, all that bollocks." Jez joined in, not one for traditional birthday greetings. "How old are you today?"

"Twenty-eight," Alfie replied. "Always said I'd be married by the time I was thirty but I can't see me settling down for a long time yet."

"You never know, mate," I chipped in. "You might meet the woman of your dreams and become a happily married man with a few kids one day. You just never know what's around the corner." I took a swig of the beer.

"Bloody hell, Gaz, what's come over you? Got something to tell us?"

"I'm going out tomorrow night. Taking Janice from Jack's cafe to Luciano's." Jez and Alfie choked in unison.

"Fuck me, fella, what you taking her there for? Why don't you get a burger and go to 'dogger's beach' like you usually do?"

"Because Janice is a classy bird, that's why. I think she's used to being treated properly. I can't see her being impressed with a night at McDonald's and a shag in the back seat."

"That's what you usually do, innit?" Alfie was enjoying himself now.

"Not anymore it isn't. It's time I met someone with a bit of...finesse, someone I can spoil. I don't expect Janice to sleep with me on our first date."

"Well, rather you than me. She sounds like someone you'll get bored of, Gaz. Not your type at all. And taking her to a posh place for a first date is setting her sights a bit high. What happens on your second date when you've got no money and she won't settle for a Big Mac?" In hysterics, Jez had to put his can on the table and his slice of pizza back on the plate for fear of messing up my mum's sofa.

"Don't know why I bothered telling you two. After Saturday night's fiasco I'm surprised you're not riddled with something."

"I tell ya, Gaz, that Julie was well up for it. They didn't go home till three, we were knackered. I reckon the girls could have kept going longer but I had to chuck 'em out in the end."

I tutted and took a bite of pizza. "I can't believe you set me up like that." Not wanting to get into a conversation about their shenanigans I laughed, hoping it would make them see that I was over it.

"Fancy trying again this weekend?" Alfie was staring straight at me.

I looked at Jez then back at Alfie, noticing a smirk appear on both their lips. "Just kidding, mate. We saw how uncomfortable you were, though I don't see why when you spend half your life at 'dogger's beach'."

"*Did* spend half my life there, Alfie, *did*. If it works out with Janice tomorrow, I'll be a changed man. I really like her, have done for a while and I don't intend cocking it up."

"So you'll be a one-woman-man then?" Jez had an element of shock in his voice.

"Yeah, that'll be me." I took another bite of pizza and thought about Lisa for a moment, wondering if I should mention her as well. But then thought better of it when I realised my new one-woman-man character was in danger of falling at the first hurdle if I did go out with Lisa on Saturday.

"How's it going at work, Gaz?" Alfie asked. He enjoyed listening to my tales of college, mainly because he'd spent three years there, playing the field and getting acquainted with almost every female in the building, including a few members of staff.

"I got a new job offer today. Kevin's offered me the Head of Communications post. Joe Mint's decided to retire and they reckon I'd be the best man for the job."

"Isn't Joe Mint that horny bugger who got caught with his trousers down with Jane White?"

"Yeah, he's the one."

"What happened to her? I heard she moved away because her family were ashamed. Can't believe he was never sacked over that." Alfie had been mates with Jane White, in fact I think he'd made a play for her mum once and got knocked back.

"They were a nice family and I think they were really embarrassed about it. Joe was let off because the college couldn't afford to lose him at the time."

"So how come he's decided to retire? He's only in his forties."

"He's been at it again," I said, realising I shouldn't have and was in danger of breaking confidentiality rules. "Do you remember that little blonde sort in the main office, Harriet Bell?" Alfie was thinking. "Attractive woman, probably mid-thirties, bit ditzy." He nodded and slurped his beer. "Her husband caught them at it a few weeks ago and he's more or less been forced to leave. They couldn't sack him because technically he hasn't done anything wrong but he's agreed to take early retirement and find part-time work elsewhere, which means they need someone to take over his job."

"Good on you, mate. Are you going to take it?"

"Probably, I haven't decided for definite yet. Thought I'd have a chat about it with mum, see what she thinks. I always wanted to work directly with the students but this is more about liaising with outsiders, getting work experience for students and helping them on their way once they've decided on a career. Not absolutely sure I want to do it yet."

"More money?" Jez asked.

"Yeah, quite a bit more."

"Well, what are you waiting for, you knob? Take it, snatch their hands off. From the sounds of it, you'll need every penny you can get your hands on with this new bird of yours."

"Janice isn't like that." Not sure why I was defending her because the truth was, I didn't really know what Janice was like. "I'll keep my options open where birds are concerned."

Alfie and Jez laughed. "See, you'll never be a one-woman-man, Gaz. You like variety. Treat 'em mean, keep 'em keen, that's what you always said."

"Yeah, well, let's wait and see what happens tomorrow. It might go tits up and be a disaster, then again it might not. No one knows what's around the corner."

"Drink your fucking beer, mate, you're boring my tits off with all this monogamy shit." Jez had a way with words. Though I was damned if I'd ever let him have a way with my mother.

Chapter Six

Wednesday night finally arrived and I had a shower, shave and chose a nice pair of jeans and a beige shirt. Even my unruly brown hair seemed to behave itself when I smeared a finger-tip of gel on the top. I left a bit of stubble on my face, though not enough to cause a rash on Janice should I have got lucky. I'd been like a dog with a bone all day at work and hadn't had chance to think about Kevin's offer of the new job. The only thing on my mind had been picking Janice up and enjoying a night at the restaurant with her. The fact mum had given me £50 to use was a bonus and I decided to draw out another fifty to make sure I had plenty of money in my wallet when it came to paying the bill.

The car started first time and I could have kissed it. When I got to Janice's road, a tree-lined avenue with huge houses set back, many behind electronic gates, I started to panic, realising I could have been biting off more than I could chew. Reviewing the road she lived in she was probably used to dining at posh restaurants and having guys spend a fortune on her. I pulled up outside her house, 'Duchy House' as it was called, judging by a large slate plaque stuck on to the gate post. I got out of the car and made my way nervously towards the drive. I noticed a curtain twitch in one of the downstairs windows then the front door opened and a man who looked in his fifties stood there, hands in his pockets, watching me as I walked towards him.

"Gary?" he said, holding out his hand for me to shake.

I took his hand and his almost crushed mine in the firmest handshake I'd ever experienced. I suspected he was a mason. "Yes. Is Janice ready?" I wasn't sure if he expected me to address him as 'sir' but I stood my ground, making him see that I wasn't some puny no-hoper just wanting to bed his little girl then dump her in the recycling bin.

"She is, yes. Why don't you come in for a moment then you can meet Janice's mother. We've heard a lot about you." I felt I had no choice, especially as Janice was nowhere in sight.

Feeling a bit awkward I followed him into the front room, a large oblong lounge with high ceilings and a chandelier. There were photographs everywhere, mainly of Janice, some of her mum and dad in evening wear. My first thought when I entered the room was 'I hope I haven't got dog shit on my shoes', a strange thought by all accounts but the house seemed so pristine it would have been my worst nightmare to walk muck on the carpets.

"Delia, this is Gary, the young man who's taking Janice out tonight." Delia, whom I suspected was Janice's mum, came towards me, a huge smile imprinted on her attractive face, her hair in a bun, looking quite glamorous I have to say. I held out my hand and she took it.

"Nice to meet you. I hear you're taking Janice to

Luciano's. Jack and I go there regularly, it's our favourite restaurant in the area, though you can rest assured we won't be encroaching on your date tonight, ha-ha."

Feeling awkward again, I withdrew my hand from Delia's, not knowing what to say and wishing Janice would get a move on. It was just at that moment she walked through the door and literally took my breath away. Her dazzling smile melted me on the spot and apart from the cleavage that was obviously on show to tease me, I knew I was smitten and was sure this would be our first of many dates. She was stunning in a pale blue dress, matched with dark blue stilettos, and her hair almost identical to her mother's, tied up in a bun with a few wispy bits hanging loosely by the side of her face. I walked towards her and gave her my biggest smile, reaching out for her hand and lifting it to my mouth. Right then, I couldn't have cared if Alfie and Jez were standing in the room, I just wanted to spoil this girl who stood in front of me and show her that I was a changed man. A one-woman-changed-man.

"Shall we go?" I asked, in my most gentlemanly voice.

"We'd better had. Did you book a table?" she asked.

"Yes, for seven-thirty."

"Have a lovely time, dear," Delia said, watching as her daughter glided into the hallway. "

I turned to face Janice's dad. "We won't be late, sir," I said, then felt like a right knob when Janice giggled her way to the car.

I opened the door for her and waited until she'd got in, gently closing it behind her. Then I walked round to the driver's side and gave a little wave to her parents who were still standing at the front door, looking like they were waving off their newly married daughter. A few butterflies were doing the rounds in my stomach as I turned the engine, hoping to god the car would start first time. Much to my relief it did, and I carefully drove us to the restaurant, parking up behind it in one of their designated spaces.

"My dad said you must have a really good job to be taking me here on our first date." Janice smirked as we got out of the car. "I told him you work at the college."

"Well I do," I replied, "though my job isn't the best paid job in the world by a long shot."

"I'd have been happy going to the pictures you know, you don't need to impress me by bringing me here." She hesitated at the entrance.

I opened the door and allowed her to walk through but she stayed glued to the spot. "Aren't you going in then?" I asked.

"Are you sure you want to spend your money in here?"

"Of course I'm sure." I beckoned her to walk in front of me and closed the door behind us. No sooner had the latch fastened on the door, a smartly dressed waiter came over to us and offered to take our coats.

"This way sir, madam, your table is ready for you." He led us to a candlelit table for two in the corner of the restaurant, an opulent yet intimate space with a dozen covers, most of them taken by posh-looking diners. There were silver wine buckets by the sides of the tables and soft Italian music playing in the background. I have to admit I didn't feel altogether comfortable but I wasn't going to let Janice see my nerves.

"Can I get you a drink, sir?" The waiter said, bending slightly as he spoke. He looked at me, a white linen cloth draped over his arm.

I looked at Janice. "Ladies first," I gestured, and she ordered a glass of house red wine. I ordered the same and the waiter tottered off leaving us to peruse the menu's he'd handed to us as we sat down.

I tried not to look at the prices but couldn't help notice the cost of a bowl of soup at £9.50. I went for bruschetta followed by spaghetti bolognese, not too expensive considering some of the other choices, and Janice chose garlic mushrooms and Steak Diane. I decided to relax and not let the cost worry me.

"This is nice," Janice said. "Have you been before?"

"Never. My mum and dad have been in here a few times but they never brought me."

"Same here. This is one of dad's favourite restaurants, I think that was why he was so impressed when I told him you were bringing me here."

"So he wouldn't have been as impressed if you'd have said we were going to Burger King?" Janice laughed and shook her head.

"I can't believe you called him 'sir'. He's quite down to earth really you know, just likes to assert his authority. I haven't had many boyfriends mainly because he scares them off, but I could tell he liked you. I'm sure he won't mind if you call him Jack."

"What does he do?"

Janice looked at me as though I was a bit thick. "Well, what do you think he does? He owns a chain of cafes in the North East. Jack's? Jack's cafe? Where I work?"

The penny dropped and once again I felt like a right knob. "Of course, you work for your dad then. Good job to have. Guess it's steady enough."

The waiter came back with two glasses of red wine.

"It's okay, though I don't see myself working there for much longer. It's just a stop gap until I go to Australia. I'm trying to save some money up, then I don't need to rely on dad to..." I'd stopped listening when she mentioned 'Australia'.

"Are you going for a holiday?"

"No, I'm going to live there. I've wanted to live there for three years now and I've just never done anything about it, but mum and dad said they'd support me and would give me their blessing if I really wanted to do it.

Dad quite likes the idea of setting up a franchise in Sydney so I'm going over there with that in mind."

I couldn't have felt worse if Bethany Calder's brick-shit-house boyfriend had punched me in the knackers. I took a large gulp of wine and swallowed it, nearly choking as it roughly scrambled its way down my throat.

"I didn't realise you were moving to Australia," I said feebly. "When do you plan on going?"

"Not for a few months yet. I've got my Visa and can go anytime now but I'm giving myself a little bit of extra time to save up then I'll be on that plane, destined for a new life in the land of barbeques and surf." She looked towards the ceiling with a dreamy expression. "God, I can't wait to be honest."

All I could think was this date was going to be the first and last I'd have with Janice. There would be no point taking her out again if she was buggering off to the other side of the world. And a part of me wished I'd taken her to Burger King.

"What about you, will you stay working at the college?"

I thought about that for moment. "Yes, I expect so. I've been offered a different job this week, kind of a promotion. Think I'll probably accept it as I do like working there."

"That's good, congratulations. Will it mean more money for you?"

"Yeah, quite a bit more really. Might mean I can afford to move out of mum's though I reckon she'll try and talk me into staying."

"Aww, you live with your mum, how cute." Janice giggled again and I felt like a loser. I think she must have noticed my deflated expression and added, "Well I live with my parents as well so I know how you feel. It's good to be independent but it's good to have someone fuss over you isn't it?"

"Oh yes, mum is always fussing over me but she does

let me live my own life as well. I can't say I don't enjoy living there, but my mates have their own places and I think it's time I thought about it, too." I'd been thinking it was time for me to get my own place for years but I did like the attention mum gave me, not to mention the fact she waited on me hand and foot.

The starters arrived. I expected a bit more food for the money I was paying but the taste was superb and presentation second to none. I could see why it was one of the best places in Bedworth. Not sure I'd want to go back though.

"How are your mushrooms?" I asked, noticing how Janice was cutting them in half so as to fit them into her dainty mouth.

"Mmm, delish," she replied. "What about your bruschetta?"

"Best I've ever tasted I reckon. Could have done with a bit more though." I sniggered and Janice looked over at my plate, nodding her head.

"I know what you mean. Bit stingy aren't they? That's the problem with these posh restaurants. They charge you an arm and a leg and you need a fish supper on the way home." We both laughed as the waiter came over and asked if everything was to our satisfaction. In true British fashion, we both nodded and grinned like Cheshire cats.

"I can't believe you haven't got a boyfriend," I said, looking into Janice's eyes. "You look stunning tonight."

"I used to go out with a guy from the hairdressers in the precinct. We were together for about three years."

"What happened, if you don't mind me asking?"

"No that's okay. We just drifted apart really. Our relationship was going nowhere and I could tell he didn't want to carry on seeing me so I just told him we should finish. I'd never seen him looking as relieved as he did when I said that. You might know him actually, Sean Gray, from Hatley, senior stylist at Jennies."

I did know him and thought he was a right tool. "Yeah, I know who you mean. Tall guy, loves himself."

Janice laughed. "That's him. He's a good looking bloke but everyone seemed to fancy him and I got fed up every time I went to see him at work and found a client flirting with him. He would never have cheated on me but I guess we just weren't right for each other in the end. I heard he got engaged recently, to one of his clients." She sniggered when she said that and I was quite taken with her blasé attitude.

"Better off without someone like that I reckon. You deserve much better."

"Aww, thanks Gary, that's a lovely thing to say. What about you, have you got a girl in the wings?" I wasn't sure why she was asking as I'd brought her to a posh and expensive restaurant in the hope of making *her* my girlfriend. I wondered if she'd got the wrong idea and assumed I just wanted to be friends.

"No one," I answered. "I've had a few girlfriends in the past but nothing serious." I didn't think it was important to tell her about all the one-night-stands and the coloured drawing pins I'd pushed into a cork board to mark how many women I'd had. And anyway, I'd made a decision after Alfie's disastrous orgy that I would throw that cork board away. I didn't want to be reminded of my colourful past and my attempt at breaking the world record for shagging.

"I'm surprised you don't have someone special in your life. You're such a lovely guy." I thought I saw her flutter her eyelashes at me but I wasn't sure if it was just the garlic sauce making them water. "It's really lovely to be out with you tonight. I hope this will be the first night of many for us?"

"I guess it depends on when you go to Australia," I said, not quite knowing what had made me blurt that out, making me sound bitter about the fact I probably wouldn't get the chance to have Janice as my permanent girlfriend after all.

"Well, I'm sure we can enjoy each other's company in the meantime." I nodded at her response, grateful at least for a temporary arrangement.

"I'd like that." I finished my last mouthful and put the fork down.

"Can I take your plates, sir?" The stuffy waiter was back, completely ignoring Janice and just acknowledging me. It might have been good nosh and a very exclusive joint but I didn't like the chauvinistic attitude of the staff and vowed to myself there and then I'd never set foot in the place again.

The main courses arrived within five minutes, again quite small portions, dressed with leaves and two tiny new potatoes next to Janice's steak. She said it was delicious and walloped it down whilst I tucked into my spaghetti bolognese after the waiter had smothered it in parmesan. I ordered another glass of red wine for Janice and mineral water for me then we had a look at the dessert menu, the only thing I wanted being Tiramisu. We both ordered the same, along with an espresso then the inevitable moment arrived when I needed to request the bill. I did the usual charades where I drew in mid air on a pretend piece of paper, and the waiter scuttled off with an evil smirk, getting back to our table at record speed with a little black leather-bound flip case.

I could sense Janice's eyes boring into the case, dying to know how much it was. I opened it up and glanced at the total amount, feeling relieved when it wasn't as much as I'd expected. There was only a couple of pound's change from sixty quid so I left the cash in the case and passed it to a waiter saying quite confidently, "keep the change." No one came back to the table and when we got to the front door we had to find our own coats from the stand, fumbling about through fur and leather to get ours. I suspected the waiter wasn't impressed by my measly tip but I couldn't care less.

They were rude and I was still hungry.

I was tempted to stop off at the chippy on the way back to Janice's house and buy a fish supper. Nice as the food was in there, the portions were definitely not value for money. As we drove through town the smell of fish and chips and kebabs was wafting into the car and my stomach started to rumble. I noticed Janice look out of the window at one point; I suspected she was embarrassed about my lack of anything to say, or maybe she was hoping I'd pull over for a fish supper, too.

"Would you like to go anywhere else?" I asked, as we came to a T junction. Left would be Janice's road and right was towards 'dogger's beach', though I was quite sure she wouldn't have wanted to go there.

"I don't mind. I did tell my dad I wouldn't be too late but we could perhaps stop at Clowns for a nightcap?"

Clowns was one of my favourite bars in town but it was one I frequented with Alfie and Jez and I wasn't too sure I wanted to walk in there with Janice, running the risk of them taking the piss. They would only embarrass me and I was trying to get to know Janice on a friendly level, rather than our usual 'how long till you got into her knickers?' level.

"How about we stop off at the George instead, it's usually quiet in there during the week." Janice nodded and smiled, she was quite easy to please.

I pulled over outside the pub and applied the handbrake. "I'm having a lovely evening," she said, staring straight into my eyes. I wasn't sure whether she was waiting for me to kiss her but I unclipped my seat belt and got out of the car instead. It wasn't that I didn't want to kiss her, I did, more than anything right then. But I didn't see the point in getting too close to her knowing that within a few months she'd be living on the other side of the world and I'd never see her again. I went round to her side of the car and opened the door for her, unable to take my eyes off her cleavage as she bent to get out. She seemed to exaggerate the bending bit but I didn't mind. The stirring in my trousers wasn't too bothered either.

The pub was thankfully quiet and there were plenty of tables to choose from. We found a little round table in the corner, a comfy sofa wrapping around three-quarters of it and a stool on the other side. I got us a couple of drinks at the bar then we made ourselves comfortable next to each other on the red velvet, Janice's body pushed up against mine. It was a very pleasant feeling, especially when she put her hand on my thigh.

"I thought you'd have wanted your wicked way with me tonight, Gary," she said, much to my surprise. "But I reckon I've scared you off with my news about going to Oz."

I wondered if she were a mind-reader. "No, not at all," I lied, on both counts. The thought of taking Janice and her cleavage to bed excited me beyond belief but it seemed different with her somehow, not quite so rushed. I didn't feel a hasty need to get her into bed. I just wanted to woo her for a bit before I did.

"I was warned about you. I was told that you've had a lot of girlfriends and you're on a mission to get as many girls into bed as you can, before you're thirty." Who the fuck had she been talking to, I wondered. Alfie and Jez didn't know her so it couldn't have been either of them.

I laughed. "Good god, no, where did you hear that?"

"Billy, in the cafe, he said you see yourself as some kind of stud and I should be careful or I'll end up another notch on your bedpost."

Bastard Billy Brown, I would give him a piece of my mind tomorrow. "I think he fancies you," I responded, smirking and drinking my J20 at the same time, half of it dribbling down my chin.

"He does fancy me, he always has. But I don't fancy him you see, and never will. He's a good friend but that's all and he drives me mad sometimes with his jealousy. I just wish he'd stop trying to control me." Janice looked into her glass of red wine with a slightly sad expression.

"Are you afraid of him?"

"Oh no, he's a pussy cat. But he's a bit obsessed with me at the same time. He promised my dad he'd look after me while I work in the cafe and my dad took that to mean he'd watch out for me, you know, in case of any difficult customers. But I've noticed recently he's started putting customers off coming in. We used to get lots of students coming in at lunch times, boys mainly, year threes I think, and I do enjoy a bit of a flirt with them. But Billy scowls at them so much that they haven't been in for months now."

"What a barrr...stool," I said, remembering to watch my language in front of a lady. "He has no right to intimidate you and he certainly has no right to put customers off. Have you told your dad?"

"No, there's no point. I'll be out of there by summer and I'll never see Billy again. I feel a bit sorry for him really, he doesn't have a girlfriend because he's always working, and when he's not working he's at home studying for his degree."

"What's the degree?"

"Psychology. He's quite an intelligent bloke but he does think he's clever and can, you know, read people." She chuckled and took a swig of wine. "He makes me laugh though, he can be really sweet sometimes."

I didn't like Billy Brown. "I don't think it's sweet to try and control you, that's just mean."

"He cares about me, and I can't ask for more than that. Like I say, we've been friends a long time." She shuffled on the sofa and moved her hand a bit further up my thigh towards my crotch, making me stir. "Gary?"

"Yes, Janice."

"Do you want to sleep with me?"

"What do you think?"

"I think you do."

"Do you want to sleep with me?"

"What do you think?"

"I reckon so."

"Is there anywhere we could go?" The tips of Janice's fingers were now stroking the growing bulge in my pants and she licked her lips a few times in readiness.

"My mum's out tonight, we could go back to mine if you like?"

"But then you'd have to take me home again."

"That's okay." She knocked her red wine back in one gulp and I slurped my J20, disguising the gas as I stood up and wrenched the car keys from my coat pocket.

It didn't take long to get home and I was glad my mum had decided on a late night at Claire's. She wouldn't have bothered about me taking Janice back but it was much nicer having the house to ourselves when we walked through the front door. Janice took her coat off and stood in the hallway, waiting for me to take off my jacket. Before I knew what was happening she was wrapping her arms around my neck and kissing me, hammering her lips against mine, her tongue exploring my tonsils. Janice was up for it and so was I.

It took about five seconds to get our clothes off and climb into my bed. She didn't even comment on the bomb site that was my room. All she seemed interested in was a good seeing to and getting well acquainted with my cock that fortunately stood very much to attention and did me proud. I fancied Janice more than I'd fancied any other girl I'd taken to bed. This girl was different, more refined, sexier and more sensual than any of the others. She knew how to please me as though we'd been together for years. She knew all the right places to put her tongue and exactly how long she could get away with teasing me before I'd need to let off some steam.

The cleavage was still magnificent when I took her bra off. I rubbed my face against her breasts and softly caressed her nipples with my tongue feeling ecstasy beyond my wildest dreams. Janice was hot, she was completely going for it, not letting up for a second. There was no shouting and screaming from her, just moans and a few oohs' and arh's. She didn't need to yell 'fuck me' or 'do it' to get my attention, she had me like putty in her hands. I turned her over and parted her legs a little, not needing to do much work because she was ready for me to enter her and give her the ride of her life.

Janice climaxed at exactly the same time as me, it was like our orgasms had been synchronised. She wasn't just another notch on my bedpost, she was '*the*' notch on my bedpost because I couldn't imagine ever having sex with another girl like that again. Nothing could surely compare to Janice. She lay beside me, her breasts rising with every breath, a smile etched on her beautiful face as she turned to look at me.

"Wow, you're amazing. That was perfect." She ran her nails down my arm, sending more shivers cascading around my body, arousing me for round two.

"*You* were amazing, Janice," I replied, and I meant it. She *was* amazing. She was stunning and incredible and everything I wanted in a girl. I turned on my side and touched her breasts, running my fingers over her still-erect nipples. I leant towards her and kissed her softly on her lips. "I wish you could stay here tonight."

That was when she turned and looked at the clock on my bedside table, before jumping up and grabbing her underwear that she'd thrown on the floor.

"You'd better get me home, or my dad will be wondering where we are."

It was eleven o'clock and I figured it probably was time to end the wonderful evening, but I grabbed her and pulled her back onto the bed, kissing her lips and fondling her breasts, just one last time.

"Can we do this again?" I asked, as I withdrew and started to get dressed.

"Of course we can. But not Luciano's if you don't mind, I'd rather just get a take away and come back here."

That was the best suggestion I'd heard all night. "Didn't you like it there?"

"Oh yes, it's a beautiful place, but it's so expensive and I'm starving."

I laughed. "Me too. Shall we stop off at the chippy on the way back to your house? We can eat them in the car if you like."

She fastened the buttons on her dress, the cleavage just poking out, smugly teasing as my eyes rested on it. "No, I need to get home. Besides, I don't want to go home stinking of chips do I?" Good point, I thought.

We arrived back at Janice's just before half-past eleven. The outside light was on and what looked like lamplight in the front room, but there didn't seem to be any other signs of life. Janice leant towards me and kissed my lips, lingering just long enough to make the kiss feel comforting and not like one of those 'see you around' types.

"Thanks, Gary, I've had a wonderful night."

"Me too," I said, planting another kiss on her mouth. "When can I see you again?"

"I'm in the cafe every lunch time during the week so you can always see me there. Maybe we could arrange something for the weekend?"

I suddenly felt a very uncomfortable cartwheel in my stomach as I remembered Lisa Hill and my potential date with her on Saturday. That couldn't possibly happen now, I'd have to tell Lisa our date was off. Whether I'd have the guts to tell her why was another matter, but before I could answer Janice, she gave me another kiss then got out of the car, closed the door and ran towards her front door. I watched her fumble for her house keys and let herself in, and then I put the car into gear and slowly drove away. Deciding to worry about Lisa tomorrow at work, I got home and climbed back into bed, feeling somewhat lonely on my own, missing Janice's warm body against mine and her soft kisses on my neck.

Chapter Seven

"Gary!" Shit, it was mum. I'd over-slept again and she was knocking on my bedroom door, ordering me to get my lazy arse out of bed before she came in. I'd slept like a log, drifting off to sleep with thoughts of Janice's breasts against my chest and her mouth wrapped around my cock. But it was now eight o'clock and I needed to be up and out in half an hour.

I had a quick shave, splashed some cologne on then dressed in jeans and a dark blue shirt, grabbing a slice of toast that mum was holding out as she stood at the bottom of the stairs. "You'll lose that bloody job one of these days," she said as I ran out the front door. "And drive safely."

"Later, mum," I shouted as I got to the car.

Unfortunately, I arrived at the college just as Lisa was turning into the car park. Knowing she'd wait for me, I tried to put off for as long as possible the inevitable walk into college together. She'd obviously got the impression we were an item because she linked her arm through mine and gave me a little peck on my cheek. I pulled away, not wanting to give her the wrong idea.

"What are you doing, Lisa?" I asked, half laughing, half mortified.

"Just thought I'd show you how happy I am to see you. They'll all know soon enough."

"Who's they and what will they all know?" I asked, not laughing anymore.

"Our work colleagues, they'll soon know that we're seeing each other. I've already told Nettie and Olivia that we're going out on Saturday night and they're really chuffed for me. They know I've liked you for ages."

Bollocks, I wasn't going to get out of this one as easily as I'd first thought.

"Anyway, you're not embarrassed are you? I don't embarrass you do I?"

I turned to face Lisa, realising my hostile mood was offending her. "No, of course I'm not embarrassed. And you certainly don't embarrass me." I smiled, kicking myself in the head and threatening to have words with myself when I was alone in my office.

"I'm really looking forward to Saturday. Where are we going?"

I quickened my pace, forcing Lisa to unlink her arm. She tried to keep up beside me as I neared the main entrance and even though I felt like a right bastard, I honestly didn't know what to say. I really didn't want to take her out anymore and couldn't believe she assumed we were together. I couldn't stop thinking about Janice and wondering how she would feel if she found out I was arranging a date with another girl. My reputation would precede me and I was trying to change my ways.

"Look, Lisa," I began, "can we talk about this another time, I've got tons of paperwork to do." I looked at her, noticing a split second of anger in her eyes.

"Fine, I suppose I should get to class too. How about lunch today?" I wanted to go to Jack's cafe to see Janice so I shook my head.

"Sorry, no can do. I'm meeting a friend in town."

"Well, why don't you ring me tonight? Here's my number." She started scribbling on a piece of paper then passed it to me. "I get home after six, going to the gym after work today, need to keep in shape now that I've got myself a fella." She chuckled and tottered off, her backside wiggling as her stiletto heels clattered along the corridor. I shoved the bit of paper into my pocket and made my way to my office, closing the door behind me and standing against it for a minute with my eyes closed, wondering how I'd given Lisa the impression I was her 'fella'.

Just as I sat down at my desk the phone rang. It was Kevin Holloway, asking for a decision.

"Thing is, I've heard someone else might be interested if you're not so I could do with your answer by the end of today. Have you had a think about it?"

I hadn't really thought about it properly, having other things on my mind like Janice and her cleavage for one, not to mention Lisa's obsession with me.

"Yes, I'll take it," I said, not really sure where the words came from but relieved I'd given him my answer.

"That's great, Gary. I'll get the contracts drawn up and inform HR. Joe leaves in two weeks but it'd be a good idea if you touched base with him so he can show you the ropes. Maybe get yourself sorted for Monday morning, would that suit?"

"That's fine, Kevin. I'll make sure I don't make any appointments next week." What I wanted to say was, 'let's hope none of the students need to discuss their future prospects', but I thought better of it. The guy had just promoted me and the few extra thousand a year would come in very useful, especially if I was going to move out of mum's.

Kevin hung up and I sat and stared at my desk, looking at the mish-mash of papers strewn over the surface, some that needed attention, others than needed throwing in the bin. I couldn't wait to tell Janice about my new job, then realised I should probably tell my mum first.

I went to Jack's cafe that lunch time, mainly to see Janice. I felt a bit awful when Lisa was watching me out of the window, blowing me a kiss as I walked out of the college gates. But I was just glad she wasn't following me, which was something that had crossed my mind earlier. I arrived at Jack's to see Janice serving a good-looking guy with a coffee and Billy doing his usual impression of a Kray twin as she seemed to flirt with the customer over the change. She laughed and closed the till then looked my way and mouthed 'Hi'.

I sat at a table against the wall and she walked over to me. I noticed the glow on her face and a twinkle in her eyes, and when she put her hand on my shoulder a warm glimmer penetrated my whole body.

"I was so tired this morning," she said, almost in a whisper. "I really enjoyed last night."

"So did I. And I over-slept this morning. Mum was banging on my bedroom door." Janice giggled. "Could I have a chicken and mayo roll today please, and a pot of tea?"

"You can have anything you like," she said with a mischievous grin. "Would you like some dessert?"

"In here?"

"Yeah, I'll put it on that table over there." She indicated to a long oblong table on the other side of the cafe.

"Doesn't look very comfortable to me," I grinned.

"It doesn't need to be comfortable, I don't intend lying on it, just leaning against it." She looked straight into my eyes, hers unflinching. My cock was in danger of poking through my trouser pocket at this rate.

"You're insatiable you are," I laughed.

"And you love it, don't you?"

I shook my head and continued to laugh. "You'll have Billy Brown seething over his shortbread if you don't pack it in."

"I told him I'm seeing you."

"What did he say?"

"He tutted and said I was stupid. So I told him to mind his own business. He says you'll break my heart but I told him he should find himself a nice girl and settle down." She started to walk away. "I'll have a think about dessert," she said, winking at me over her shoulder.

My chicken and mayo roll was ready but unfortunately, Janice had to serve another customer which meant Billy brought it over to me. I examined it as he was putting it on the table, making sure he hadn't spat in it or anything. He had a very serious look on his face and the protective side of me just wanted to punch him.

"You hurt her and I'll be after you." He said it with a sadistic smile on his face as though he enjoyed making threats to innocent people. "I know about your reputation and she's too good for you." He stood next to me with the tray in his hand and lowered his voice. "I'm warning you, I'll fucking kill you if you hurt my Janice."

Was he for real? What an arsehole, and who the fuck did he think he was by calling her 'my Janice'? Idiot. The sooner Janice was away from him the better. But then the awful realisation struck me that the only reason Janice would be away from him was because she would be emigrating, and would therefore be away from me too. I tried not to relish that thought too much and picked up the chicken roll, taking a large bite as I watched Billy stroll back towards the counter where

Janice was flirting with another customer.

By the time I'd finished my pot of tea, it was getting time for me to make my way back to college. Janice came over to say goodbye and I glanced over her shoulder to see Billy watching our every move. Just to annoy him I decided to lean in for a kiss, which she obligingly gave me. Shove that up your arse, Billy Brown, I thought as I walked towards the door.

I realised I was being childish but I wasn't having the likes of Billy threaten me with violence when Janice wasn't even his girlfriend.

That night I rang Alfie and told him about Janice and how Billy had acted like a tosser.

"He's a nasty bastard him, mate," Alfie said. "He's been inside for GBH." Great, I thought, just what I need, a broken nose to look forward to once Janice finds out about my new status of being Lisa's 'fella'.

"Yeah well," I began, cockily, "he doesn't scare me. I really like Janice and she likes me so he can just fuck off."

"What about the other bird who fancies you, the one with the nice tits?" He meant Lisa. He'd already met her a few months ago at a staff member's birthday party I took him to. It had been a great night in all honesty but Lisa had followed me around the room like a lap dog and when I introduced her to Alfie, I noticed he couldn't take his eyes off her chest.

"Hmm," I replied.

"What do you mean 'hmm'?"

"Bit of a problem there, mate. You see Lisa thinks I'm taking her out on Saturday night. She's got the impression we're, err, together like." I had to take the phone away from my ear whist Alfie composed himself after laughing hysterically down the line.

"So you're not a changed man after all. Fucking hell, mate, that didn't last long."

"I am a changed man. I don't want to take Lisa out,

she's not my type. She just got the wrong impression, that's all."

"So you're not taking her out then?"

I hesitated. "Well, I suppose I'll have to really, I mean, she's dead excited about it and I thought I might take her for a quiet drink and let her down gently."

"Got a way with birds you have, Gaz. So the poor girl will get herself all dolled up for you, probably put her best thong on and then you'll tell her you're not interested. And you value your knackers do you?" Alfie started laughing again.

"I'll tell her tomorrow that it's off."

"Yeah, whatever, mate. I'd keep your options open if I were you, go out and enjoy yourself. You might find she's a goer."

"I'd say she's definitely a goer," I grinned, thinking about Lisa's pert breasts and those visible nipples that always seemed to show through her blouses.

"Well don't be a dick then and get in there."

It was a decision I knew I'd have to make and sooner rather than later but I hung up the phone when mum came in and followed her into the kitchen.

"Empty the bags for me, son," she said, putting them on the table. "My feet are killing me. These bloody shoes have been rubbing all day." I reached into the Morrison's bags and started putting stuff in the fridge whilst mum sat at the table and rubbed her ankles.

"I've got some good news, mum," I said.

"You tidied your room?" she grinned.

"Not today, but I will." She laughed and shook her head. "I've got a new job at the college, a promotion, more money."

"Bloody hell, son, that's brilliant. You didn't tell me you'd applied for a new job. When did this happen?"

"Kevin Holloway offered it to me at the beginning of this week but I wanted to have a good think about it before I said anything. Anyway, I gave him my answer today and I start in a couple of weeks."

"Well, I'm really pleased for you. You've been doing the same job for a while now haven't you? A change will do you good. What's the job?"

"Head of Communications." It sounded good when I said it out load, especially the Head bit.

"Ooh, sounds posh. What will you be doing?"

I told mum a bit about the job description and she seemed really impressed. I was always pleased when my mum was happy.

"Will you be able to give me a rent increase then?" Damn, I hadn't seen that one coming.

"How much, like?"

"Another tenner a week?"

"Ten?" I gasped.

"Times are hard, Gary, and it sounds like you'll be earning more than me now. Good god, lad, if you lived on your own you'd be paying a damn sight more in bills than you do now." She had a point, so I agreed an extra ten pounds a week, wondering how the hell I was supposed to save up and buy my own place one day. "How did it go with that girl last night, did you enjoy yourselves?"

The thought of Janice brought a smile to my face. "Yeah, we had a good night."

"What about Luciano's, how did you find it?"

"Hmm, pricey, but nice food. Not enough on your plate though and the waiters are a bit rude."

"That's what I used to think but your dad thought it was the bee's knees. Did you go anywhere afterwards?"

"Just for a quick drink to the George." I thought better of telling mum I'd brought Janice back here, mind you, it wouldn't surprise me if Mrs Dean from next door hadn't already told her.

"Well it sounds like everything's coming together for you, son. It's about time you had some good luck in your life. I hope you'll treat this girl right and not use her for sex."

"Mum!"

"What? I'm a woman of the world, I know how your minds work. I was your age once you know."

"Yeah, and you were happily married to dad at the time."

"Aye, and look where that got me. I suppose I might as well tell you while we're on the subject, I'm going out with a fella on Saturday night, Terry Whitehouse from work. He's asked me out a few times and I've never felt it was right but I'm sick of being on my own, son, and I reckon I should have some fun before it's too late. Are you okay with that?"

I looked at mum. "Why are you asking me? So long as he treats you right and you're happy, that's all that matters to me. Where's he taking you?"

"We're going to the Brewer's Whistle. It's Terry's sister's fortieth and he's asked me to go with him."

"Sounds nice. So you'll be meeting his family as well?" I sniggered.

"Yeah, looks like it. Thing is," she paused, "Terry's a bit younger than me." Mum looked a bit sheepish.

"How much younger?"

"He's 38." Mum stood up and went to the kitchen sink, her back to me.

"Bloody hell, mum. That's a big age gap."

She turned around to face me. "It's not that big, you cheeky bugger. I'm only 51."

"That's thirteen years. He's thirteen years younger than you. Isn't he married?"

"No, he isn't married. He got divorced a few years ago and lives on his own. He's a lovely man and I like him a lot. I'm not moving in with the bloke, just going on a date with him." She opened the cupboard and took out a pan. I thought she was going to hit me with it for a moment. "And anyway, you can talk. Remember that floozy you went out with last year, Deborah Carnivore?"

"Deborah Carnival," I corrected her. "And it was only a few times."

"How old was she? Definitely older than me, I'm sure. And if she wasn't she looked it."

"Deborah was forty-five and had a body like a woman twenty years younger."

"That's because she works at the leisure centre gym. She's bound to have a figure like that when she's working out all day, every day."

Deborah gave me the green light the moment I walked into the leisure centre. I was only going in for a swim and ended up humping her over the rowing machine after hours. Jez and Alfie thought it was priceless when I told them about her, couldn't believe I'd had her of all people.

"Is she up for it?" Alfie had asked when I was bragging about my conquest in the pub.

"Yeah, I'll say. I'm seeing her again tomorrow for another session."

"You lucky bastard," Jez chimed in. "I've wanted to take her out for ages. I've spent a fucking fortune at that gym and every time I go she's never working. I was hoping she'd do my induction." He gyrated as he said that, causing Alfie and me to snort our beer.

"Well anyway," mum said, "that age gap was bigger than mine and Terry's, so you can shut up and be happy for me."

"And are you going to introduce him to me at some point?" I was in danger of sounding like my mother when I'd told her about Janice.

"I'll see how it goes on Saturday night first and if we hit it off then I'll invite him round for a curry next week and you can get to know him." That was fair enough, I thought. Mum knew she didn't need my approval if she wanted to date some guy, but I appreciated her wanting my blessing.

"So will you be late in on Saturday then?" An idea

was racing through my head.

"Probably. Terry's picking me up at seven and I don't imagine I'll be home before midnight. These dos tend to go on till about one don't they, and they've got an extended bar on." She poured some oil in the pan. "Have you got plans?"

"I might have, not sure yet."

My plans were to bring Lisa back here and not risk being seen anywhere else, like in town where we could very well bump into Janice. I could order a takeaway and we could just sit and talk, listen to some music. And maybe I could pluck up the courage to tell her about Janice and that I was sorry for misleading her. Yes, it was best to let her down gently in familiar surroundings. At least that way she wouldn't clobber me in a public place and make me look like the idiot I am. I congratulated myself on the marvellous plan I'd devised then thanked mum for the ham and cheese omelette she put in front of me, along with the can of Fosters.

Chapter Eight

*T*he following day was Friday, the day before I'd once again break a girl's heart and make myself look like the biggest arsehole that walked the earth. I tried hard to avoid Lisa, realising I'd forgotten to ring her last night, but she collared me as I walked through the main entrance. I reckon she'd been waiting for me. She was wearing some red skinny jeans and a very tight t-shirt that I thought was a bit inappropriate for work, but then I realised it was none of my business what she wore. She was a flirt, always had been and I suspected always would be. The fact that she had now deemed me to be her 'fella' wouldn't make the slightest bit of difference to Lisa and what clothes she wore; whoever her fella was would just have to put up with her ways. For a second or two I had a mad thought that perhaps I could accuse her of being unfaithful to me and say I didn't trust her, but when her nipples were once again thrust towards me, the hormones took over as did the thought of what she might be capable of in bed.

I shook myself off and walked towards her, smiling

and trying not to make it obvious I was enamoured by her chest. She came at me with puckered lips, her arms outstretched, but I managed to dodge the embrace, pointing out that we were at work and there were students about.

"Oh, you're so bashful. Live a little. The students are up to all sorts. I've caught them many a time going at it behind the kitchen bins." Who said romance was dead?

"Yeah, well, we're in the front entrance not behind the kitchen bins, I don't feel comfortable fiddling with each other in public."

I noticed a sulky expression suddenly appear on her overly made up face. "From what I hear, it's never bothered you before."

I laughed and opened the double doors that led to my office. "I've grown up since," I said, wishing she wasn't following me.

"Let's go into your office and lock the door. I'll let you take me over the desk." If that had been Janice I wouldn't have hesitated.

"Don't be daft," I said, finding this changed man a bit surreal. "I need to get to work. Lots of queries to sort through today."

I quickened my pace as my office door came into view. "Gary," Lisa purred, waiting for me to turn around and face her.

Unable to resist, I looked at her just as she was licking two of her fingers. "I've got no knickers on."

My thoughts raced around the fact that a beautiful and sexy woman was standing in front of me in a college corridor telling me she was knickerless. I swallowed and looked at her crotch. I had to resist. I couldn't let Lisa have her wicked way with me over my desk, a desk that would one day be used by someone else when I'd taken over from Joe Mint. But no undies? Now that was tempting.

"Did you hear what I said?" she asked, her hand now

playing with the pendant that just rested on her cleavage.

I cleared my throat and composed myself. "Yeah, I heard you, and I reckon so did half the college. I'll see you later, Lisa, okay?" I turned around and strutted towards my office, congratulating myself at resisting an urge that in any other circumstances I wouldn't have ignored in a million years. I heard Lisa tut then turn on her stiletto heels, striding back towards the double doors.

Walking into my office, I closed the door and leant against it. This was becoming a habit, me leaning against my closed office door, abstaining from Lisa's offers of sexual contact. My growing erection was telling me a different story however, obviously disappointed at my new-found character. I'd already risen more than was acceptable in a work environment and so I quickly sat down and shuffled some of the papers on my desk, determined to beat the bulge.

By lunch time I'd more or less sorted out the form filling, tidied up files and taken two phone calls from irate parents about their troubled teenagers who were talking about dropping out of college and needed my expert opinion.

"Rupert is so bright," Mrs Granger said in her posh accent, not at all in-keeping with our local northern twang. "His father and I told him last night that he should speak to you before he makes any rash decisions. He has his whole future in front of him and both Henry and I want him to go to university, Edinburgh preferably as he's always been good with animals and we think he'd make a wonderful vet."

"Mrs Granger," I started, wondering if she'd ever sat and talked to her son. "The last time I spoke to Bear, err, Rupert, he expressed a very keen interest in being a chef. He's doing very well in his studies but I honestly don't think the course he's currently doing is the right one for him. I really think you ought to speak to him about it."

"But we want him to be a vet and we know he's capable. Why, only last week he was diagnosing our neighbour's cat with flu and then the week before that he helped deliver a litter of puppies. He's far too bright to be a chef," she said, quite rudely I thought. It dawned on me that I wasn't getting anywhere and her precious son would need to either follow his dreams and drop out of college or carry on with his course and spend the rest of his life studying and doing a job his heart would never be in. It always made me feel bad for the students when they had pushy parents. At eighteen years old they should have been able to make up their own minds what they wanted to do with their lives, but so many of them didn't have a clue.

I made a mental note to speak to Rupert that afternoon and warn him that his mum had been on the phone and would want to talk to him about a possible career change over the weekend. I felt sorry for the poor lad, he certainly did have the makings to be a vet, he was definitely intelligent enough, but the fact his heart was in catering was going to mean he had a very big decision to make, and one he'd have to make sooner rather than later, if not just to shut his snooty mother up.

I decided not to go to Jack's cafe at lunch time as I was starting to feel bad about Janice and the fact she had no idea of my potential rendezvous with Lisa. Instead I went to see Lisa in her classroom who was standing at the white board, wiping the writing away. Her face lit up when she saw me hovering at the door, making me feel even worse.

"Gary," she exclaimed. "Come in. Do you want to go out for lunch?"

"No, I've brought some sandwiches." She seemed a bit disappointed. "Unless you do?"

"No, it's okay, I've got sandwiches too. Just thought it might be nice to go out together, you know, maybe to the pub or somewhere."

"Another time perhaps? I haven't got long." That was true strictly speaking, though I could have taken the full hour's lunch break and worked a bit later that afternoon.

Lisa took a plastic Tupperware container from her bag and sat at a student table, pulling up the chair and beckoning me to sit down next to her.

"What have you got?" she asked, examining my white doorstops and packet of prawn cocktail crisps.

"Cheese and pickle."

"So where do you want to go tomorrow night?"

"Well, I was thinking perhaps just a pizza and a bottle of wine at my place?"

"Seriously?" Lisa put her sandwich down and ran her fingers over her coke can.

"Unless you want to go out somewhere? I just thought it would be quieter, we could talk, you know."

She winked. "Talk? Yeah right. I know your game, Gary Stringer, you want your wicked way with me don't you?"

I took a bite of my sandwich, chewed it and nodded my head. "You know me well, Lisa." I shoved the sandwich back into my mouth, anything that would prevent me from speaking again.

"You'll need to give me your address."

"Number twenty, Waterfall Gardens. It's the new estate on the edge of town."

"I know it. Shall I bring an overnight bag?" Blimey, I thought, slow down.

I pondered that for a moment, opening the crisps and shoving a handful into my mouth, munching them noisily. "Well, my mum will be back before midnight," I lied, hoping Lisa would get the hint.

"That won't matter will it? I bet you've told her all about me."

"To be honest, Lisa, I haven't told her about you," I hesitated, "yet." Nice one.

"Why not?"

I smiled at her innocence. "Well, I think we should get to know each other first, before we start introducing each other to our parents. We are grownups after all."

Lisa smiled and took a bite of her sandwich.

"And besides, my mum is going on a date tomorrow night and I don't think she'll want to hear about my love life."

I think it was the 'love' bit that did it. Lisa put her sandwich on its foil, leaned over and kissed me, hard on the lips. She placed her hands either side of my face and looked deep into my eyes. "You're such a lovely man. I'm so lucky." Then she kissed me again.

I leant back in my chair, noticing the nipples again, protruding like two cherries on a muffin. I have to admit, I was very tempted to bend Lisa over the desk and have a quickie before lunch break was over but I stayed composed, crossing my legs and hoped Lisa hadn't noticed she was turning me on. The thought of her being in my bed was getting more arousing by the minute and I suddenly realised I hadn't thought about Janice since we'd sat down at the table. Maybe I did need to give this thing with Lisa a go, I mean, Janice would be upping and leaving in a few months and then I'd be left with no one. And if Lisa was as mad for me as I was beginning to suspect, I couldn't look a gift horse in the mouth now, could I?

It was almost one o'clock when I stood up and walked to the door. Lisa went back to her desk and picked up her bag, following me down the corridor towards the Ladies toilets. I made my way back to my office where I once again shut myself in, leant against the door and hoped my cock would deflate.

Chapter Nine

I woke up on Saturday morning after a restless night's sleep, tossing and turning, thinking about Janice and Lisa. I'd had a dream about Deborah Carnival at one point, she was in the Leisure Centre pool, skinny-dipping, and I dived in and swam up to her, only when I reached her it was Lisa. My mind was all over the place and I was in need of some strong coffee and one of mum's cooked breakfasts. I ventured out of my bedroom, stubbing my toe on a pair of black shoes, and then went downstairs, adjusting my tackle and yawning my way to the kitchen. Mum was sat at the table reading the paper, her hand grasped around a mug of coffee.

"You alright, son?

"Not slept well. You don't fancy making me a fry up do you? It'll make me feel better."

"Yeah, I'll make you something. Sit yourself down. Did you have a lot to drink last night?" I'd stayed in last night, sat in front of the TV with a few cans of Fosters, nipping out for the occasional cigarette.

"No, I'm not hungover, just knackered."

"You thinking about your date with Janice tonight?" mum asked, a smile on her face as though she was really happy for me. I wasn't ready to tell her about Lisa so I'm ashamed to admit I lied.

"Yeah, she's on my mind a lot right now." Okay, so it wasn't a total black lie, just a little white one, because Janice *was* on my mind, only so was Lisa and the awkward situation I'd got myself into.

"You really like her don't you? I've never known you to be so taken with a girl before, not like this anyway."

"She's a great girl."

And she was; just mum talking about her as she slapped some rashers of bacon in the frying pan was making me ache to see Janice again. I'd really enjoyed our night out and desperately hoped she'd want to do it again soon. Of course the sex was a bonus, but it wasn't the main reason I wanted to see her again, which meant my ways were definitely changing.

"Where are you taking her tonight?" Mum put the cooked bacon onto a plate and cracked a couple of eggs into the pan.

"Err," shit, I thought, this lie could become a bit grey around the edges if I'm not careful. "Not sure yet, we'll talk about it later." Thankfully, mum changed the subject as she put the plate of food in front of me.

"Get that down you, then go and get in that shower and sort yourself out."

"Cheers, mum." I picked up the bottle of tomato sauce, squirted a large dollop onto the side of the plate then buttered some slices of bread that mum had put on a separate plate.

The rest of Saturday went by in a haze and it was five o'clock when mum shouted upstairs, "What time are you going out?"

I told her it'd be about eight-ish, knowing full well she'd have been long gone by then. I'd told Lisa to come round for eight, that way I could be sat watching the Dave channel on my own by nine after having let her down gently. But it hadn't escaped my notice that due to my reaction to her rather suggestive lack of underwear at work yesterday, not to mention her amorous advances at lunch time, I was in danger of letting her down gently onto my mattress, thus creating a problem that might get out of hand if Janice found out.

Mum looked stunning when she came downstairs. She was wearing a long floaty dress and gold sandals, her hair pinned up and just the right amount of makeup on to show off her good looks. I felt proud of her as she was looking out of the window waiting for Terry Whitehouse to arrive. He drew up in his brand new Mercedes at seven on the dot. Mum did a little leap in the front room then turned to look at me.

"How do I look?" she asked, patting down her dress.

"You look beautiful, mum. I hope Terry treats you right."

"Oh he will, son. He's a nice man." Just then Terry tapped on the front door and mum ran to answer it. I heard a bit of shuffling in the hall before she came back into the front room, her lipstick smudged slightly. "Gary, this is Terry." Mum stood aside and let Terry into the room. Tall, broad, dark brown hair, he looked very sophisticated and not at all like I expected. I imagined him to be a bit scruffy if I'm honest though I don't know why. Maybe it was because dad always seemed a bit scruffy, and perhaps that's what I expected mum's type to be. But Terry was a pen pusher, I could tell a mile off. He held out his hand.

"Nice to meet you. Your mum's told me a lot about you."

I smiled and shook his hand, making sure he knew I was on his case and if he upset my mum he'd have me to answer to. "Hope you have a nice time tonight," I said, as he drew his hand away and placed it a little too familiar-like on my mum's back. I watched as she looked up into his eyes, obviously smitten.

"You have a good time with Janice, son. And if she wants to come back here to stay she's more than welcome. I'll see you in the morning." She leant towards me and gave me a little peck on my cheek then floated out of the front room, into the hallway and left the house. I watched as Terry opened the passenger door for her then closed it softly, walking confidently round to the driver's side. He did seem okay, not at all like my dad, but I imagined mum wanted a change and on the whole I was glad for her. It was about time she found herself a nice man, a companion, someone to have a little romance with occasionally. And on that note I ran upstairs and put on a bit more aftershave.

At eight o'clock I looked out of the front room window and saw a taxi draw up. Watching Lisa get out and pay the driver, I noticed she had a small hold all with her, obviously her over-night bag. My stomach flipped as I realised this letting her down gently might not go according to plan and if she'd packed a bag she was obviously expecting to spend the night in *my* bed, not her own. I panicked a bit when I went to open the front door and she skipped towards me, a huge smile on her face. I'd ordered a pizza for ten-past eight, at least that way we could eat first before I told her I didn't want to go out with her because I was keeping my options open with Janice. I'd rehearsed a little speech just in case she took it badly; I'd tell her I didn't think she wanted to actually be my girlfriend and was just after a quickie, but everything seemed to have been obliterated from my memory as she came towards me and kissed me on the door step.

"I can't believe we're alone at last," she said, as she walked into the hallway and put her bag down. Then she flung her arms around my neck and nestled into me, pushing her breasts into my chest and rubbing herself against me.

I pulled away, trying not to offend her. "I've got a pizza being delivered any minute," I said, as she stepped back. "I'll get some plates out and pour the wine."

"What have you ordered?"

"One barbeque chicken and one ham and pineapple, wasn't sure what you liked."

"I like both of those." She followed me into the kitchen. "Your house is lovely. Is this your mum?" She picked up a frame with a picture of mum in it taken a few years ago when dad still lived with us.

"Yes, that's mum."

"She's very beautiful. Doesn't look very old."

"She's fifty-one," I said thinking mum will kill me if she knows I've just said that. She likes people to think she's late thirties, not that anyone does of course as otherwise it'd make it impossible for me to be her son.

The pizza arrived shortly after and I paid the young lad whom I knew from college, gave him a tip and he told me to have a good night. I reckon he knew I'd got Miss Hill in the kitchen pouring the wine, as his smug expression screamed 'I know what you're doing.'

I sliced the pizzas up and put them onto plates then carried them on a tray into the front room where Lisa looked very much at home with her feet tucked underneath her on the sofa. I sat next to her.

"Tuck in then," I said, picking up a slice of the ham and pineapple. I'd put some music on softly in the background but was starting to wonder if I'd set the scene a bit too romantically and not enough 'let you down gently'. But Lisa seemed happy and the pizza was delicious, as was the wine, and between us we were actually enjoying ourselves.

"So, are you looking forward to starting your new job then?" Lisa asked.

"Aye, I suppose I am. I've got a meeting with Joe on Monday so he can start going through with me what my duties will be. He's introducing me to his contacts all next week so it'll be busy no doubt."

"I think it's fabulous that Kevin gave the job to you. He was going to advertise it a few weeks ago when Joe announced he was leaving, and then Joe told him you'd probably be interested."

"Yes, Kevin told me that. It was really decent of Joe, especially as he's more or less been forced to leave."

"I can't believe he's been having it away with Harriet, the dirty dog. She's a dark horse as well if ever there was one!" Lisa laughed. "You know she confided in me about their affair?"

"No, what did she tell you?"

"Only that her husband has left her. She's ended up on her own while Joe's gone back to his family and is talking of moving to the South of France. I felt a bit sorry for her really."

"Yeah, but she shouldn't have been sleeping around," I pointed out.

"Well I guess not, but Joe's wife forgave him and they're making a fresh start once he's finished at college. It's so typical that the woman comes off worse."

I snorted. "You're kidding aren't you? She got to keep her job. Look at poor Joe, been forced into early retirement. He loves working at the college."

"Maybe he does, but it was him or her, they couldn't both stay."

"So what about us?" This letting Lisa down gently might be easier than I'd first thought.

"What about us? We're single. We're not doing anything wrong."

"That's true, but really, it's nothing to do with the college if staff members are shagging."

"It depends where they've been shagging."

"What do you mean?"

"Harriet's husband caught them in the front office. Joe had her bent over the desk, was going at it like there was no tomorrow. Pants around his ankles and she was there with her knickers on the floor and her skirt over her arse. Can you imagine?" I didn't really want to imagine. The thought of Harriet's bare arse and Joe's pants around his ankles was putting me off my slice of barbeque chicken pizza.

"Oh, I see. The way Kevin told me I got the impression they'd been caught at Harriet's house, not in the office. So that's why he's been forced to take early retirement. I suppose if they'd been caught at one of their houses it wouldn't have been so bad."

"I guess not. But I think the thrill of having sex at work is immense. Don't you?"

"Shall I open another bottle?" I stood up, trying tactfully to change the subject, not wanting to get sacked for shagging at work. We'd already polished off one and I didn't want to get too drunk that I'd not be able to get my words out when letting Lisa down. I poured myself half a glass and filled hers to the brim.

She clinked her glass against mine. "To you and me, and the start of a beautiful relationship." I gulped back my wine, and then reached for another slice of pizza.

Another hour passed of small talk where Lisa filled me in on her family and her crazy brother who lived in the south. From the sounds of it he wasn't the type of person I wanted to meet having been inside for assault and arson, but Lisa said he'd changed over the years and since he'd got married and had kids, he'd mellowed. Though he didn't bother with any of the family anymore and her parents never mentioned him. Still, I was relieved he lived in the south and not around the corner or I could have come home to a burnt cinder instead of a house once Lisa had told him about her bastard of a boyfriend. But there lay the problem; I didn't want to be Lisa's boyfriend, I wanted to be her friend. It was Janice whose boyfriend I wanted to be and the more I thought about it the more I kept wondering if I should just get on with letting Lisa down and explain that I already had a girlfriend.

As the second bottle of wine was coming to an end I realised I felt a bit tipsy and my inhibitions were starting to wane a little. The thought of Lisa sitting next to me on our sofa and the fact she wanted me, was eating away as I poured the last dregs into her glass. I looked at her sat there, legs still tucked under herself, her cleavage on show and a red bra strap visible. If I was going to let her down I needed to do it now, get it out of the way before I had anymore thoughts of red lingerie and what she might be wearing underneath the jeans. Or what she might not be wearing as was probable in Lisa's case.

I put my empty glass on the table and stacked the plates up, then sat back and turned to look into Lisa's eyes. I obviously needed to work on my expressions because she took my sudden movement as a 'come-on' and leant in for a kiss. Her lips pressed hard against mine as my mouth parted. I closed my eyes and took in her sweet scent, feeling her tongue explore the roof of my mouth as she unfolded her legs and leant in further. The next thing I knew her arms were wrapped around my neck and my arms were wrapped around her waist as I helped her shuffle about and rest on top of me. She pulled her legs out and curled them around me, pushing her breasts against me.

"Oh Gary, I've wanted this for so long." Lisa was now tugging at my belt, frantic to unfasten it and obviously get into my jeans. Then she moved her hands to her blouse and undid the buttons, taking out her arms and throwing it onto the floor. The red bra was enough to take my breath away as her breasts wobbled over the cups, teasing me to touch them, which of course I did. She took the bra off and there they were, the famous nipples that I'd admired for such a long time, poking through silk blouses in the college corridors. I lifted my head and touched one of them with my tongue as she helped me slip out of my jeans. Her hand went down the front of my boxers and she started to caress me, much to my pleasure. The resulting erection was one that I was proud to call 'mine'.

"Do you want to go upstairs?" I asked, not too keen on humping Lisa on the sofa. If mum came home early she'd see us at it and not only that, I wasn't sure mum would be too chuffed to know I'd been shagging on her new settee.

Lisa reluctantly let go of my hard on and stood up, waiting for me to join her. She picked up her clothes that lay discarded on the floor then followed me upstairs to my bedroom where she looked around for a moment, probably taking in the Beirut-like atmosphere. She sat on the bed and took off her jeans, revealing the sexiest red knickers I think I'd ever seen, and believe me, I've seen some sexy underwear in my time. These had little pearls on them and lace around the crotch area. I could see a few pubes poking through the lace and it was turning me on no end. My cock was straining in my boxers, eager to explore that red lacy area and no doubt go pot holing a little later on.

I lay on top of Lisa, now dressed only in the red knickers, me in just my boxer shorts. I caressed her breasts with my mouth, my hand now making its way to Satan's alley. I was surprised at how moist she was down there, obviously ready for me to delve deeper and give her the time of her life. She threw her head back when my fingers touched her lips, and she purred "Oh God, just satisfy me." Obligingly, I did, for about five minutes before she reached orgasm and sat up, forcing me to lie on the bed so that she could taste my cock. I could tell she'd done this before, many times before, her expertise was beyond my comprehension as she thrust it into her mouth, moving that sensual tongue of hers up and down. I wanted her. I wanted to be inside her, more than anything right there and then, as I lifted myself from the bed and grabbed at her waist to turn her over. I had her over the bed, on the bed, nearly under the bed at one point when our determination threw us onto the floor in a frenzy of entangled bodies and ecstasy. She was incredible, a true expert in the field of pleasing a man. When I finally shed my load, Lisa sighed and wrapped her arms around me, kissing my chest and running her fingers around my sensitive areas.

"You're amazing," she said, lifting her head towards mine as she kissed me gently, her fingers still moving around my torso. It *was* amazing, I had to agree, and there we lay, nestled into each other like two lovers who were perfectly entitled to be nestled into each other.

I moved Lisa off me and got off the bed, reaching for my boxer shorts. "Do you want a drink?" I asked, parched and still gasping for breath.

"A glass of water please," she replied, turning onto her side and resting her head on her hand. I looked down at her and noticed the nipples, still erect and horny. I was still stirring though I felt I'd had as much pleasure as I could take for the night, so I went downstairs to get the drinks.

As I reached the kitchen my thoughts suddenly went from Lisa's erect nipples to Janice's pert breasts and the way they moved up and down after we'd had sex the other night in my bed, the same bed I'd just shagged Lisa in. I didn't know whether to be proud about the way I'd performed with two different women, or be ashamed of myself. I turned on the cold water tap and filled two glasses, turned the tap off then slowly made my way to the bottom of the stairs. There wasn't a sound coming from the house so I figured Lisa had made herself comfortable in my bed, waiting for me to get back and no doubt service her again. I was supposed to be letting her down gently and there I stood, a glass of water in each hand, black boxer shorts covering my tackle and feeling like a complete bastard.

I had a decision to make, I knew that. Two beautiful women, stunning and mad for me, great in bed, amazing bodies, fabulous personalities and both potential girlfriends. But what was I thinking? Two women in a week? I was supposed to be changing my ways, ditching the philandering, turning myself into a one-woman-man. What a joke that was. The truth was I wanted them both. I fancied them both and really, I did want Lisa to stay the night. I wanted to wake up next to her the following morning and sneak her downstairs before mum was up. I wanted to kiss her on the front doorstep and whisper "I'll call you," like I had done so many times to the notches I'd built up.

But I knew Lisa wouldn't let me get away with that. I'd see her at work on Monday and watch those nipples standing to attention as she glided towards me and I'd always remember this night of passion, a night that I knew should never have happened, but it was too late now. I looked at the glasses of water. Oh well, I thought, in for a penny, in for a pound.

Lisa was, as I suspected, tucked up in my bed, the duvet covering her modesty, though why I've no idea as I'd seen just about every inch of her. She smiled at me and sat up, lifting the pillows to make herself comfortable, her breasts flopping over the top of the duvet. I handed her the water, put mine down on the bedside table then got in the bed next to her. She took a huge gulp, put the glass down then leant into me, resting her head on my chest, her hand covering my cock. I think she might have been a bit disappointed when I didn't stir as she lifted the duvet and checked it was still there. Then her fingers started arousing me again as she wrapped her hand around it, pulling gently, sensually, throwing me into another frenzy of orgasmic bliss. I played with her for a while, satisfying her again, making me forget all about Janice and the fact I was a two-timing scum bag.

That night I dreamt that I bumped into Janice in town and she was with Bethany Calder's brick-shit-house boyfriend, looking for me. They were walking towards me and I suddenly lifted myself from the pavement and swam away, doing front crawl down Perth Street, desperately trying to get away from Janice's hit man. She was screaming at me, "you're a two-timing bastard, Gary Stringer, and we're going to chop your balls off." I woke up in a cold sweat, my nuts clenched in clammy hands and Lisa breathing softly beside me.

I hadn't heard mum get in though the smell of bacon was wafting upstairs when I eventually came round from the nightmare image of Janice waving a machete at me. Lisa stirred then opened her eyes, moving up closer towards me and snuggling herself against my chest. She was warm and soothing to the chaos that was starting to fade from my mind and a sense of pride washed over me as I looked at her face, her eyes struggling to open and face the world. I suddenly remembered the dirty plates and the empty wine bottles and glasses I'd left downstairs, fearing the worst when mum would bollock me for not clearing up before I went to bed.

"I live here as well," she always said. "You treat this place like a bed and breakfast. Have some respect." I'd heard the words a hundred times over and I never learned. Though now, as I watched Lisa slowly open her eyes and wrap her body around mine, I started to panic that mum would come in the bedroom assuming I was on my own. I shuffled towards the end of the bed and pulled my arm from underneath Lisa's warm body.

"Good morning, handsome," she said, yanking me back towards her. "Where do you think you're going?"

"My mum's downstairs," I said, struggling to get away and not doing a very good job of it. "She'll flip if she comes in my room and sees you here." Lisa sat up at that point.

"Why would she flip? Didn't you tell her I was staying

over?"

I smiled and probably looked a bit pathetic. "Well, err, not exactly," I mumbled.

"Then we should get dressed and you can introduce me to her. It'll look really rude of me if I don't go down to say hello." Lisa moved away and sat on the edge of the bed, her tits exposed. She stretched and yawned, giving my cock cause for a potential celebration but I stood up and reached for my clothes, making sure there were going to be no repeat performances of last night's passion, especially when mum was downstairs cooking bacon.

"Let me go first," I requested. "I need to tell mum you're here. It might shock her to just see you come downstairs."

Lisa, completely naked, unzipped her overnight bag and took out fresh underwear. She'd come prepared with toothbrush, make up and change of clothes. My usual girlfriends, or one-night-stands as they tended to be, would just get up and dress in the clothes they'd worn the night before, flashing a bit of boob my way for good measure, a kind of 'this is what you'll be missing if you don't see me again' gesture. I joined Lisa and got dressed, watching as she swiftly fastened the hook on her bra before she pulled on some white knickers. She put skinny jeans on and a t-shirt then ran a brush through her hair, whipped out the toothbrush and paste then hurried to the bathroom, leaving me wondering what the hell I was going to tell mum when we went downstairs.

The smell of bacon continued to waft through the house as I slowly went towards the kitchen, noticing mum dancing to a tune on the radio as she stood over a frying pan. She must have seen me through the corner of her eye because as soon as I neared the kitchen door she turned and smiled.

"Morning, son. Thought I'd make us some bacon

butties." She was in a great mood, it'd obviously been a successful night with Terry.

"Thanks, mum." I hovered near the table.

"Everything alright?" she asked, still jigging about to the radio.

"Yeah, err, everything's fine."

"Come on then, sit yourself down and I'll tell you all about my night out." Mum put the bacon on some bread she'd sliced, cut it in half then placed the butties on plates in front of me. I knew that any second Lisa would walk through the door and I'd have a whole lot of explaining to do.

"Someone stayed last night, mum."

"Ooh, you dark horse. Is Janice here?"

Just at that moment Lisa appeared at the kitchen door looking a bit sheepish, smiling as she glanced from me to mum and back to me. Mum looked at her and walked towards her, outstretching her hand.

"It's lovely to meet you, love. Come and sit down. I'll put some more bacon in the pan." Lisa and mum shook hands.

"Good to meet you too, Mrs Stringer." Then Lisa looked at me. "Gary, I'm afraid I can't stay. I didn't realise it was nearly ten o'clock. I have to get back." I couldn't have been more relieved if someone had told me I'd just won the lottery jackpot.

I stood up and went over to Lisa. "Oh, that's a shame," I lied, putting my arm on the small of her back, turning her around to face the kitchen door. "I'll take you home then."

"No, that's okay, you have your breakfast, I'll walk, it's only twenty minutes away and I could do with some fresh air."

"You're welcome to stay for a sandwich, Janice," mum called from the stove. Lisa looked at her then stared at me.

"She's hungover," I whispered, "always gets names

106

mixed up when she's had one too many." Lisa laughed, thankfully.

"Sorry I can't stay, Mrs Stringer. Nice to meet you. See you again soon." I almost pushed Lisa down the hallway towards the front door, mum no doubt looking on from the kitchen wondering why I was so anxious to get rid of her.

"You can call me Christine, love. I'm not Mrs Stringer anymore, well, not strictly. I imagine Gary hasn't ..."

I opened the front door and picked up Lisa's bag, handing it to her. "I'll tell you about my mum another time," I said, pushing her through the door. "Thanks for last night, I really enjoyed myself."

Lisa kissed me hard on the lips. "Thank you for letting me stay. I can't believe we're an item at long last." I smiled and nodded. "I'll see you at work tomorrow. Ring me later." One last kiss and she turned away and walked up the drive towards the pavement, turning back as she got to the gate to blow me another one. I blew her one back then went inside and closed the door. Mum was stood in the kitchen with a puzzled look on her face.

"Was it something I said?" she asked.

I resumed my place at the table, picking up the bacon butty and taking a mouthful. "No," I spluttered. "She had to go."

"She seems like a lovely girl. And she works in Jack's cafe did you say?"

It was time to come clean or change the subject. I nodded, not answering mum's questions but not exactly lying to her either. "So, how was your night out?" Brilliant tactic, I thought, changing the subject, take mum's mind off my inevitable confession of being a two-timer.

Mum sat at the table opposite me, a glow suddenly enveloping her. "It was such a great night. Terry's family are really nice people. They're very well-to-do, I can see where Terry gets his sophisticated mannerisms from." Job done, subject changed. "When we first arrived at the function rooms all his family were waiting for us in the foyer and each one shook my hand. His sister gave me a little peck on the cheek and said it was great to finally meet the woman Terry had been talking constantly about. I must have blushed then because Terry put his arm around my waist and gave me a little squeeze." She looked up at that point, going into a dream-like state. "We danced until the early hours, I felt like Cinderella."

"Bloody hell, mum, you make him sound like Prince Charming!"

"Well, that's exactly what he is. He's a gentleman and he really looked after me last night. I've invited him round for tea on Tuesday."

"I'm pleased for you, mum. It's about time you found someone new to spoil you. You deserve it." I finished the sandwich and slurped my tea. "I just want you to be happy."

"I know you do. And right now, Terry is making me very happy. And look at you, romancing your new girlfriend." Mum stood up and moved my empty cup. "You left that front room in a mess though." I could tell she wasn't mad with me because her tone wasn't that of a crazed woman and she didn't whack me over the head with a tea towel like she usually does.

"Yeah, sorry about that. We completely forgot about it."

She winked at me. "Don't worry. I can see you're smitten with Janice."

My stomach turned over when she said that as I thought about the fact my mum thought Lisa was Janice and I either had to tell her the truth or face the consequences from three women; one that could make my life a misery at work, one that could make my life a misery at home and the other that could poison me in her dad's cafe. I finished the last of my tea then took the cup to the sink.

"Mum, there's something you should know. That wasn't Janice."

Mum looked at me, confusion etched on her face. "What do you mean, that wasn't Janice?"

"That girl was Lisa. Lisa Hill from work."

"What about Janice?"

"Janice didn't stay last night, mum. Lisa did."

Mum picked up the frying pan and I backed towards the doorway. "I'm sorry mum, I know it's wrong and I never meant it to happen but Lisa's all over me at work and my plan was to invite her over last night and let her down gently but it never happened."

To my relief, mum put the frying pan in the sink. "Lisa from work? Well if I'm honest with you, you could do a lot worse. So where's Janice then?"

"I didn't arrange to see Janice last night. I'd arranged to see Lisa but I didn't want to tell you that because I know I shouldn't be two-timing them. Lisa thinks we're together, like properly together and I honestly don't know what Janice thinks."

"So you thought you'd keep your options open?"

"Well, yeah, I guess that's it. I'm sorry, mum, I know I'm a bastard."

Mum laughed. Last night had quite obviously been a resounding success.

"Your secret's safe with me, son. Go out and enjoy yourself before you get bogged down with a wife and kids." I stared at her, wondering if she was actually on drugs, or perhaps still drunk from her night out.

"Are you serious? You mean you're not annoyed with me?"

"It would have been better if you weren't seeing two girls at once of course, but you're young, free and single, you need to enjoy life, enjoy your freedom. Once it's gone, it's gone forever and then you'll look back on your twenties and regret not doing the things you wanted to do."

I went over to my mum and flung my arms around her, then gave her a sloppy kiss on her cheek.

"Gerroff, you daft bugger. Just be careful, that's all I ask. You get yourself in bother and you'll only have yourself to blame."

"Cheers, mum. I thought you'd want to throttle me."

"Maybe in the past I would have done, but these days, well, we have to live a little. Face the consequences if need be, but life's too bloody short."

I spent two hours that afternoon cleaning and tidying my bedroom, thinking one minute of Lisa's red bra and those erect nipples, then another minute of Janice's firm arse as I rammed her from behind. My life was pretty damn good right then and I vowed that I would keep both Lisa and Janice in it for as long as I could. After all, Janice would be buggering off to Australia in a few months so if I was careful enough, there really was no reason why either of them had to find out about the other.

Chapter Ten

I saw Janice briefly the following day during my lunch break. I didn't have long so just nipped in for a quick sandwich before getting back to Joe Mint and his disorganised filing system. There was a lot for me to learn but I felt confident that I was going to get there. His contacts had expressed regret at the fact he was leaving and there were a few emails saying they hoped his replacement would be as efficient. I vowed to prove myself to them and told Joe as much. He was a bit pissed off at the thought of retiring, mainly because he'd been forced into it.

"We should have been more careful. Let that be a lesson to you, lad," he'd said, over a cuppa that afternoon. He offered me a Rich Tea biscuit. "If it was up to me I'd still be with Harriet but her husband left her in the end and she said she wanted to be on her own. That's when I decided to stay with Sandra, see if we could make a go of what we had left. Did you know we're moving to France?"

"Yeah. How come?"

"Bloody silly bitch says everyone's talking about us and she wants to make a fresh start. They've been talking about me for years. It's got nothing to do with anyone else, they can all get stuffed. No doubt they'll find someone else to talk about when I'm gone."

Yeah, me, no doubt.

"Thing is, I do love Sandra and we've been through a lot together but I'm a man in me prime, having a bit of a mid-life crisis like. Couldn't resist Harriet and she is a sexy bugger, don't you think?"

No, I didn't.

"She's, err, very nice, I guess," I mumbled.

"She's good in bed an' all." Joe stared through the window at the green expanse of grass beyond. "Right down and dirty she is, proper goer."

"So, err, Joe, shall we get back to the job in hand?" Joe looked at me, slipping out of his comatose thoughts no doubt of Harriet bending over the front office desk.

"Gosh yes, sorry, lad, I shouldn't be telling you about my sordid secrets should I. Right where were we?"

I smiled and flicked a few papers about then picked up my pen and started making more notes, grateful that I didn't need to hear anymore about Joe and Harriet's now non-existent fling in the front office.

Jez and Alfie called round that night with a few cans. I noticed mum didn't flirt with them like she usually did and I think I sensed a little disappointment in both my friends when she left the room, announcing she was going upstairs to watch Coronation Street so we could have a boy-talk. Jez watched her walk out of the room, his eyes fixed on her backside. I cringed and shook myself off then reached for a can and opened it, taking a long swig before settling back against the sofa.

"So, you seen that bird again, Gaz?" Alfie asked. I'd contemplated telling the lads about the relapse on me changing my ways but I still wasn't sure it was a good idea. There was always the risk they'd see me with either Janice or Lisa and get the names mixed up. Mum had already got it wrong and it worried me that if someone else did the same, Lisa would start to suspect.

"Lisa stayed over on Saturday," I replied, a little coy.

"Which one's that?" Alfie asked.

"Lisa from work. The fit bird, big tits."

"Thought you were shagging the girl from Jack's?" Jez enquired, not missing a trick.

I looked from Jez to Alfie. There was no point trying to keep my secret. Plus, I enjoyed the street cred.

"I am," I replied, taking another swig of lager.

Alfie scoffed. "So you're shagging them both then? Together?"

"Not together, no. Just keeping my options open."

"That Lisa from the college is nice. I've seen her a few times when I've been there, dropping off stationery when Tod's been off. I wouldn't mind giving her one, mate." I was actually surprised Alfie hadn't at least tried.

"She is nice. I like her a lot. But I like Janice too, she's the one who works in Jack's. I don't like stringing them both on but what's a bloke to do when he can't make up his mind?" We all laughed though I knew underneath I was dicing with death.

"Exactly, Gaz. Keep it up. We have to make the most of being bachelors, enjoy the pussies whilst they're still purring."

Jez looked over at Alfie. "And what about you," he said, "have you seen that Cath bird since the other weekend?"

Alfie shrugged. "Nah. Bit too full on, if you know what I mean. Been around the block too much."

"And you haven't?" Jez laughed.

"Not like her I've not. All right for a one nighter but not the sort you'd want to take home and meet your parents."

"I can definitely vouch for that, mate," I joined in, remembering how I'd thought Julie was quite a nice girl until she revealed she was into orgies and made no bones about taking her kit off when we got back to Alfie's on that disastrous Saturday night. "Reckon she'd have given you something. Better off steering clear if you ask me."

"So what about Lisa Hill? She's been around the block a bit. I heard she was up for anything." I glared at Alfie. After spending the night with Lisa and seeing how affectionate she was I didn't want to believe that she'd been around. I knew I was wrong in keeping my options open but I wasn't too happy about the thought of Lisa and her nipples being touched by all and sundry.

"You haven't had her," I mocked.

Jez looked at Alfie. "Yet," he sniggered.

"Keep your hands off her. She's alright underneath. Even if she has been around a bit she's now with me, and I'm not having you two pawing at her."

Both Jez and Alfie held up their hands in defence. "No worries there, mate," Alfie said. "I've no intention of stealing a mate's bird." I looked over at Jez.

"Me neither," he said. "She's all yours. I just hope the other one doesn't find out soon or you'll be left on the shelf again. Honestly, Gaz, you need to be discreet this time. Plan where you're taking them well in advance so you don't bump into the other. It'll be just your luck to see one of them when you're out with the other."

He was right. I'd got myself into a situation and the biggest part of me was excited. But there was a small part of me that was terrified, especially as Lisa could make it very difficult for me at work if she found out about Janice. And the thought of Billy Brown coming after me if I broke Janice's heart had been niggling at the back of my mind. Alfie had told me he was a nasty piece of work and up until my night with Lisa I hadn't let it affect me. I'd never been scared of another man in my life and I wasn't intending to start with Billy Brown. But the fact remained that he'd threatened to kill me if I hurt Janice and the look in his eyes told me he wasn't kidding. Discreet was what I needed to be; I had to start taking Janice to places outside town where neither of us knew anyone.

It was midnight before they left and I almost had to force them out the door. Mum came down to say goodnight and seemed to linger a bit longer than was necessary in the lounge, staring at Jez as he kept his eyes on hers. I knew what he was thinking; he'd always liked older women and after mum telling me that Terry was much younger than she, I was starting to wonder if mum did actually fancy Jez. It was a bit worrying, having one of my best mates and my mum flirting with each other, and the fact I knew Jez's reputation made it even more so. I made Jez promise that he would never make a move on my mum and he laughed at me, calling me a soppy bastard, saying I was too much of a mummy's boy. Maybe he was right. Maybe I was a bit of a hen-pecked son but since dad had left, my mum had been lonely and deserved someone to take care of her, not someone to treat her like a one-night-stand then dump her the next day.

On Tuesday night I got in from work to the smell of chicken curry and mum standing at the oven, stirring a pot with a wooden spoon. She looked flustered as I went into the kitchen.

"You alright, mum?"

"Oh, this bloody curry isn't thick enough. I tried to make it from scratch but I've buggered it up." She replaced the lid then put it back into the oven. "Terry will be here at six and it's already half-five."

"Have I got time for a quick shower?"

"Yeah, but don't mess the bathroom up, I've cleaned it this afternoon." Mum generally only cleaned the bathroom if we had visitors, and special ones at that. Usually, I just cleaned up after myself or let mum give it a quick wipe round. She refused to clean the toilet after I'd been on it, saying I was as bad as my dad for splashing.

I ran upstairs and stripped off then had a quick shower and a shave, spraying myself with Lynx. It was almost six o'clock when I went downstairs again to see mum setting the table in the dining room. We usually ate on our knees or at the kitchen table; the dining room was kept for birthdays and Christmas and the occasional special guest.

"Are you trying to impress Terry?" I asked, sniggering when I saw the best crystal wine glasses.

"Course I bloody am. Go and get a bottle of white wine from the fridge and put it on the table, he'll be here any minute. I want him to see that I've made an effort." I did as I was told and fetched a bottle of Sauvignon Blanc, placed it in the centre of the table and put the corkscrew next to it. Seconds later the doorbell rang. "Shit," mum said, "how do I look?"

"You look gorgeous. Now go and answer the door and stop acting like a teenager!"

Mum looked in the hall mirror, ruffled her hair, smoothed down her dress then composed herself before she opened the front door. I heard her say hello to Terry who in turn told her how beautiful she looked. That would have been at least ten brownie points for Terry, a good move on his part. They walked into the front room where I was stood waiting. Terry held out his hand and I shook it.

"Hello again, Gary. Hope you didn't mind me encroaching on your evening?"

"Not at all, Terry. A friend of mum's is a friend of mine." God, I sounded like my granddad.

"Let me take your coat, Terry," mum said, fussing him as he undid the buttons then slipped it off his shoulders. He handed it to her and she scurried off to the cloakroom. "Gary will open the wine," she called.

I moved into the dining room and picked up the corkscrew and the bottle. "You didn't need to go to all this effort, Christine. A pizza would have done me." I liked Terry already.

"Nonsense," mum said, standing at the door and throwing her hand in the air. "It's nice to cook something special." She looked into Terry's eyes. "*For* someone special," she added. He grinned at her and twitched his nose. I looked away for fear of barfing into the nearest bin.

"Go and sit in the front room with Gary and I'll finish off the dinner." Dinner? I thought. It's usually tea. I couldn't help but snigger as I poured the wine and handed one to Terry.

"Cheers," he said, "good health and all that." I nodded my head and took a sip, trying not to look uncouth as I wiped away a dribble from my chin. "Good stuff," he said. "One of my favourites."

"So what's your job at the supermarket then, Terry?" I thought I should act interested, after all, I wanted to make sure mum was getting involved with someone high up the ladder.

"I'm the manager of the store, have been for a few years now." I was impressed. Mum seemed to know what she was doing. "It's a great job, very diverse. Something different happening every day which keeps it interesting. And then of course there's the staff." Mum walked in the room as he said that. "Like your mum for one." He winked at her and she rolled her eyes at him.

"I hope you're hungry both of you. There's a mountain of food."

"Good, I'm starving," I said, going to stand up.

"Five more minutes, son. Keep Terry entertained

while I get our prawn cocktail ready."

Prawn cocktail was reserved for a *very* special occasion. Mum had definitely pushed the boat out here and I thought it was time I started getting to know Terry a bit better just in case their relationship was about to turn serious.

"Do you have any kids, Terry?" He must have thought I was a right knob head when he snorted wine out of his nose and almost choked.

"None that I know of," he chuckled eventually, once he'd wiped wine from his top lip and composed himself again. "I was married for a few years but it didn't work out. We drifted apart and felt it was better we went our separate ways." He took a sip of wine and put his glass on the table. "You've no need to worry. I am very fond of your mum and have no intention of hurting her. We're just getting to know each other and we intend on having a good time doing that. I know you're very protective of her since your father left and believe me, so am I."

"She seems very fond of you too," I said, staring him straight in the eyes.

"I've wanted to ask her out for a while now but I've always held back because I know she's older than me and I honestly wasn't sure she'd take me seriously. But I've always felt older than my years, and to be honest I see your mum as someone much younger than a woman of fifty-one."

"She likes to think she's younger than fifty-one," I laughed. "Maybe she's having a midlife crisis."

Terry glared at me. I got the impression he didn't like the thought of my mum having a midlife crisis and him being the main attraction.

"I don't think so, though you obviously know her better than I do. We're genuinely fond of each other and I hope our relationship progresses." He picked up his wine glass and took another sip. "Of course, with your blessing."

I looked away. I wasn't used to these types of formalities where I was expected to give my blessing for a relationship my mum was about to embark on. It should have been the other way round. Fortunately, mum saved me from embarrassing myself and announced that dinner was served. Terry shot out of his chair like a rocket and went into the dining room, examining my mum's culinary skills. I have to admit it looked fabulous. Her prawn cocktail was superb and the table was very expertly decorated. She'd even put napkins by each place setting; we usually make do with a sleeve.

"Christine, you've gone to an awful lot of trouble, this looks amazing."

I looked at Terry as he and mum swooned at each other. Starting to feel like a gooseberry, I quickly sat down and began tucking into my prawns. Terry pulled out his chair, made himself comfortable and laid the napkin on his lap. I think my manners probably left a lot to be desired as he looked over at me as though he couldn't believe I'd started before mum sat down. All this pomp and circumstance just wasn't something I was used to, and to be honest I wanted to finish my meal as quickly as possible so I could bugger off upstairs and leave mum and Terry to continue swooning at each other in private.

"Were you hungry?" mum asked, looking at my empty plate.

"Starving." I replied, filling my wine glass up.

I wondered what Janice would make of this as I imagined her being used to these types of dinner parties where guests were invited and the family sat around the table politely chewing their food and making courteous remarks about the meal being exquisite. I was missing her. I'd fully intended to go into the cafe at lunch time that day and ask her out again but Joe had other ideas. He insisted that I accompany him to the White Horse where he bought me lunch and a pint of beer. It was, admittedly, a very nice lunch and we had a great laugh but part of me really wanted to stop by the cafe and see Janice.

I wasn't sure what to make of these feelings I was experiencing because I was trying really hard not to get too close to Janice when all the time the thought of her moving away was niggling at the back of my mind. I'd even thought briefly about not asking her out again and just leaving it at that one date, but the truth was I did enjoy popping into the cafe for my lunch and the thought of seeing her smiling face as she walked towards me made butterflies soar in my stomach. It was like she was my drug; I needed her but didn't want to get addicted.

Mum shot me a look. "Gary, will you go and open another bottle of wine please?" I stood up. "And take your plate with you."

What was it with mothers, I thought, the minute they get a fella they start treating you like you're ten years old. I grabbed my plate and the empty wine bottle then went into the kitchen, quite glad to get away from the table for a few minutes, and the virtual juices that seemed to be flowing. I was thinking seriously of asking mum if I could eat my main course in my room but thought better of it when I plonked the fresh bottle of wine on the table and she looked at me again with that 'you dare embarrass me and I'll kill you' look.

When I'd finally finished my main course at the table and listened to Terry compliment mum on everything from the salt cellar to the curry strength, I leant back in my chair and patted my stomach.

"That was delicious, mum," I said. "Would you mind if I left you to it? I've got a bit of paperwork to get through for a meeting tomorrow morning." I think that impressed Terry because he looked at me with a dazzled expression. Mum looked at Terry and I assumed it was for approval.

"Sounds like you're enjoying your new position at the college. Your mum told me about you changing your job, getting a promotion."

I nodded. "I'm enjoying it so far though got a lot to learn about the job yet. It'll take a while I expect."

"Well you certainly sound dedicated to it. I like that. So many young people these days seem to think the world owes them a living." Who the fuck did he think he was, I thought, the Prime Minister?

"You're not that old yourself, Terry," I said, a little too smugly and mum shot me another one of her 'I'm going to kill you' looks.

Fortunately he laughed. "Sometimes I feel twenty years older than I am, at least. Being the manager of the store is a very demanding role but it's an enjoyable one I'm glad to say. I wouldn't want to do it if I didn't enjoy it."

"Terry works extremely hard," mum said. "I don't think people who work there realise just what he does in a day. The responsibility is immense."

"Yes, it is, Christine, especially when we get staffing issues as well. I seem to be at everyone's beck and call and I've got quite a few supervisors who don't seem to be able to think for themselves. It can get very tiring at times. But like I say," he looked at me again, "I do enjoy the job and wouldn't have it any other way."

I'd actually liked Terry when he first arrived but now I was starting to err on the side of thinking he was a knob. I stood up and left the room, leaving him to impress my mum with his 'I'm indispensable' bollocks.

My bedroom was a welcome distraction and even though I'd lied about having paperwork to do, I did open up the book that Joe had given me and read through some of the job description. I'd taken the job and was determined to make a go of it. The last thing I wanted to happen was to fall flat on my face and find that if I failed at being Head of Communications, there wouldn't be a job for me at the college anymore.

It was half-past ten when mum shouted up the stairs to tell me Terry was leaving. I thought it only polite to say goodbye and so went down and shook his hand whilst he stood in the hallway.

"Very nice to spend time with you. I can see why your mum is so proud of you." His firm handshake was making me feel like I'd been on trial.

"Yeah, likewise," I said, prising my hand from his. I noticed mum was ecstatic with pride and I also noticed she looked a little flushed around the cheeks. It didn't take a genius to guess that they'd been intimate on the settee, the same settee that I'd been intimate on with Lisa the other night. That thought sent shivers down my spine.

I retreated back to my room and closed the door, hearing whispering going on downstairs then the front door being bolted. I couldn't make up my mind about Terry, whether I saw him as a potential long term prospect for mum. I still worried about the age gap, hypocritical as it was, but I'd have been deeply pissed off if mum was falling for him and he decided on a younger model. I just wanted her to be happy.

I got to work early the next morning simply because I couldn't stand listening to mum singing 'Can't Smile Without You' one more time from the kitchen. I decided on grabbing a sausage roll from the college canteen just to save me having to go into the kitchen and being greeted with a manic woman dancing to her own out-of-tune rendition of one of Barry Manilow's finest. As usual, Lisa collared me as I was walking along the corridor. She was looking pretty damn sexy actually and a part of me felt a little protective of the cleavage she had on show, far too much for my liking. My eyes naturally averted to it as I watched the top of her breasts wobble about. She had red lipstick on too, a sure sign that she was dressing to impress.

"How's it going, Gary?" she asked.

"Great," I responded, trying really hard to stop my wandering eyes being locked onto her chest.

"Fancy meeting up tonight? I've been feeling horny for you all week." She was stood so close to me now I could smell the lipstick.

"Yeah, I'd like that."

"Shall I come round to yours again?"

I thought about that for a moment and considered her spending the night, me having to introduce her properly to my mum. Even though mum had more or less approved of my philandering ways, I wasn't sure I trusted her not to mention Janice, and if she did, Lisa was bound to cotton on. After all, mum had called her Janice the other day when she briefly saw her from the kitchen. Lisa was very much on the ball and didn't let anything get past her. In fact, I was amazed she hadn't quizzed me further about it.

"My mum'll be in so maybe we could go to yours?" I pleaded with my eyes, touching her arm and once more trying hard to drag my eyes away from the cleavage.

"I think your mum's really nice. It'll give me chance to get to know her."

I needed to think fast. "Mum's got visitors tonight so the house will be a bit crowded if we're there as well." Nice one.

Lisa thought for a moment. "Oh, okay. You come to mine for about seven. I'm not a very good cook so maybe we could get a takeaway?"

"I'll pick something up on my way." We agreed on an Indian and I walked away feeling relieved that we could be alone again in a place where no one knew me, and more importantly, where no one would see me and report back to Janice.

I arrived at Lisa's just after quarter past seven. She was standing on her doorstep with her arms folded, obviously ready to scold me for being fifteen minutes late. I passed her the brown paper bag with our Indian takeaway and leant in for a kiss but she snubbed me and turned around to walk back inside. I wouldn't like to have seen her if I'd been half an hour late. And besides, it was the takeaway's fault, there was a long queue.

"Beer?" Lisa barked at me.

"I've brought some with me," I said, as I pulled them from behind my back.

"Why were you late?"

I stared at her. "There was a queue in the Indian. It wasn't my fault. I'm only fifteen minutes late." I chuckled and tried to make light of the situation. Lisa wouldn't look at me but just dished out the food, handing me a fork.

"I thought you might have turned up early actually, you seemed pretty keen to come here when we arranged it before."

"I am keen. Is everything okay?"

"Just feeling a bit tetchy. Pour me some of that wine will you." Not sure where the lovely Lisa and her purring had gone but this was a different person altogether. I put it down to PMT.

She handed me a plate of food then stalked into the lounge. "We can eat on our knees, hope that's okay?"

"I do that most nights." I smiled and followed her to a large room painted red with a sash window in the centre of one wall. A huge bookcase dominated another wall, littered with books, DVDs and a spider plant. I sat down on the sofa expecting her to sit next to me but she chose to sit on one of the armchairs, putting her glass of wine on the floor.

"Thanks for picking this up," she said, tucking in.

"That's okay." The atmosphere was strained to say

the least.

"Do you fancy me?"

I looked at Lisa as she continued to eat her food. "Of course I do," I laughed. "I wouldn't be here if I didn't, would I?"

"I get the impression you see our relationship as a joke. I don't think you feel the same way about me as I do about you. I'm right, aren't I?"

I put my fork down and took a swig of beer. "I think we need to get to know each other, Lisa. We've only been out once and this is only our second date. Maybe we should take things a little slower."

"What, like you just want to take me to bed once a week? Are you planning on staying tonight?"

I hadn't brought a change of clothes. "Well, I wasn't going to. I have an early start tomorrow and prefer to get an early night."

"That's what I mean though. I thought you might want to stay over and we could go into work together tomorrow."

"Well, maybe another time." She was making me feel uncomfortable. She was also making me feel like a complete twat. It was Lisa's body that attracted me to her and I did fancy her like mad but I also knew that her feelings for me went way deeper than mine did for her, and right then I thought that would always be the case. I took another swig of beer, hoping it might relax me a bit.

"I've fallen in love with you," Lisa blurted out.

My only thought was 'fuck'. This wasn't what I wanted to hear at all. The word 'love' didn't exist in my vocabulary when it came to girlfriends. I was young, free and single, a guy on a mission to have the most fulfilling life I could before I was too old to enjoy it. Falling in love? Not for me. I looked at Lisa and took another swig, this time glugging back the rest of the can. I felt I deserved it.

"Aren't you going to say anything?" she asked. I

could see tears forming in her eyes as though she knew what I was thinking. "I don't expect you to say you're in love with me, if that's what's on your mind?"

She must have been psychic.

"Lisa, I'm not sure what to say."

She stood up and put her plate on the table, then knelt down in front of me, putting her hands on my legs.

"I know you don't feel the same way. I've been trying desperately to get these feelings out of my head but I can't. I'm happy when we're together and every time I see you at work my heart skips a beat. I can't help feeling like this." She fluttered her eyelashes at me and gave a weak smile. All I could do was put my empty can on the table and scoop her off the floor, into my arms and kiss her. It was either that or run a mile, which was something I was very close to doing.

She pulled away from me and took a deep breath. "It's okay," she said, "maybe one day you'll feel the same way but I know for now we should just enjoy what we have." She carried on kissing me, pushing herself into me, her hand resting on my cock as it stirred.

I moved my hands to the buttons on her blouse and started to undo them. She lifted herself off the floor and sat astride me, her kisses coming fast and furious as I continued to expand inside my trousers.

"Oh Gary, we're so good together." Lisa pushed me back onto the sofa and unfastened my jeans, putting her hand down my boxer shorts and slowly massaging me in expert fashion. I could tell it was turning her on even more as she thrust her nipple into my mouth and her breathing became heavy, a few moans escaping as I tore the blouse from her back and threw it onto the floor.

A few minutes ago I was ready to down tools and run for the hills after hearing a woman say she was in love with me. Now I was ready to saddle up and enjoy the ride of my life in paradise with a cleavage pressing against my face. She sure knew how to please me, I had no complaints there.

Within seconds her bra was off as were her skinny jeans and she was now stepping out of her knickers, discarding them onto the floor. It seemed more exciting this time, maybe it was the thought of being in Lisa's house on her sofa that was doing it, but for some reason the thought of her sat astride me and her breasts jumping up and down as her body moved rhythmically to mine was pleasuring me more than I'd ever known. This woman wanted me, every part of me, and right then I wanted her too. Thoughts of Janice had disappeared and I didn't once think of the implications that this sexy woman would have on my life. The fact was, Lisa's body was incredible. *She* was incredible and even though I couldn't bring myself to fall in love with her, I fancied her more than I'd fancied anyone for a very long time, even Janice.

Maybe once Janice had gone to live in Australia, I would eventually fall in love with Lisa but there was no way I wanted that thought to harbour for more than at least one second. That was something I didn't want to contemplate, not yet. Lisa was a very sexy woman and someone whom I knew I could probably be happy with, but tonight had also shown me that she had an insecure streak, a side to her that I found a little tiresome. I'd been fifteen minutes late and had received the third degree as though she thought I was being unfaithful, or didn't care about her enough. I wasn't ready for that. I wasn't sure I ever would be.

Chapter Eleven

I think Wednesday night was a success in the end. Lisa's mood seemed to shift once we'd finished having sex as we lay on the sofa, arm in arm. She snuggled into me and switched the television on so at least it took my mind off thinking about that 'love' word again. I didn't want her to keep telling me she was in love with me, it just felt too heavy, and I'd never been a guy to do all the deep and meaningful stuff. I left her flat at midnight after the film we watched finished. A part of me did want to stay the night but I refused to let myself be talked into it. Though I'll give Lisa credit, she tried very hard.

"Aww, come on. It'll be amazing, you here with me and then us going to work together tomorrow."

"I can't, Lisa, I'm sorry."

"But don't you want to wake up next to me again and let me set you up for the morning?"

"I can't, Lisa, I'm sorry."

"I'll make you breakfast in bed, bacon butties, just how you like them. And I'll give you a blow job for afters." I have to admit I was tempted. Bacon butties had always been my favourite breakfast.

"I can't, Lisa, I'm sorry."

"Will you stay over another night?"

"Definitely. Will you make me a bacon butty and give me a blow job if I do?"

She leant over and startled fiddling with my cock again. "You don't need to ask that."

Suffice to say, I was knackered the next morning at work and mum had to almost bang my door down to get me out of bed. Lisa's parting blow job was a blow job too many for one night, but she sure knew what she was doing.

College was buzzing that morning. Students seemed to be everywhere, carrying files and laptops, chatting and laughing in corridors. It was like an echo going on around me as I struggled to remember whether it was Wednesday or Thursday. I settled on Thursday after asking Jane McNewby as she lazily pottered passed me, not a care in the world, probably thinking about the job she'd have at the end of her course that daddy would hand to her on a plate. She was one eighteen year old that irritated me; completely spoilt, bad mannered and arrogant. Her attitude was 'My family's got money and I couldn't give a shit about anyone else.' I'd had a run in with her once and realised just how much of a bitch she could be.

"Jane," I said quietly, as she'd pushed in front of me at the canteen. "There's a queue here."

"And?" My hackles rose.

"Get to the back of it," I said, a little louder.

"I'm busy. Some of us have work to do, you know."

"I don't give a flying fff...," thought better of it as she *was* a student, "fadoodle if you *do* have work to do, so does everyone else in this queue, including me." I glanced at the other students in the queue, all of whom were engrossed with their mobile phones.

"You teachers think you're so superior," she smirked.

"For your information, I'm not a teacher, I'm a career's advisor."

"You're still a staff member of this college and without students here you'd be out of a job. You especially."

That did it. Apart from throttling the little bitch, I looked around, realised that everyone was now staring at me, and decided to stand my ground. "Who the hell do you think you are? Just because you're one of the lucky ones with a job to go to once you've left here you think you're a superior being. Well let me tell you something, Jane McNewby," I was really going for it now. "You're no better than anyone else. You've been born with a silver spoon in your gob and you should think yourself lucky that you have parents who are willing to give you a chance in their firm. Most students at this college don't have that kind of luxury and actually have to work bloody hard for their future." The next thing I heard was Jane ordering a bacon butty before thanking Edna, the canteen lady, and strolling past me as I carried on ranting. "When I was at college, which wasn't that long ago, I had to work very hard to get a good job and it's made me all the more appreciative of it..."

"Mr Stringer, what can I get you?" Edna was standing in front of me with her hands on her hips. I turned around to see Jane McNewby at the canteen entrance with her mobile phone stuck to her ear, laughing loudly as she cradled the bacon butty. Never again would I speak to that girl, not even if she wanted careers advice.

Joe wasn't in when I walked in to his office, the one that would soon be mine. There was a note on the desk telling me he'd be late and I needed to arrange a couple of meetings with the local hairdressers to get placements for work experience week. It was too early to ring them so I sat at the desk and opened the newspaper. It was almost nine o'clock when Lisa breezed into the office, her radiant smile cheering me up after I'd been reading about some nutter who'd set fire to his shop. Lisa walked over to the desk and perched on the end of it. Her breasts looked particularly splendid in the tight-fitted Lycra top she was wearing, the nipples once more on parade.

"What do I owe this pleasure?" I asked.

"Just wondered what you were doing this weekend and if you fancied staying over at mine." It was a tempting offer. I nodded.

"That sounds good to me, though I'm not sure if Alfie and Jez wanted to go into town at some point."

"I was thinking you could stay the whole weekend. Come to mine after work on Friday and we could go out for the day on Saturday, have a meal out then have a night of passion, and you can go home on Sunday some time." She stood up and started walking towards the door, her tight little bottom forcing my eyes to look down. "But if you'd rather spend time with your mates, I'll find something else to do."

"No, I'd like to spend the weekend with you. I'm sure the guys will understand."

She turned around and smiled at me again. "Have you told them about me?"

"Yeah, course I have." I hadn't exactly told them about how close we were becoming, a little too fast for my liking.

"That's great. Maybe we could meet up with them on Saturday night and you can introduce us."

Stopping myself from jumping out of my seat and expressing a very loud 'Whoa, hang on', I smiled and instead suggested we spend the weekend on our own so we could get to know each other better. I winked at her as well which made her come over to me and run her fingers down my cheek. An erection was just starting to grow when the door opened and Joe walked in. Saved by the Mint.

"Hi Lisa," he said, a little too cheerfully. "What's going on here then?"

Lisa bent forward and kissed me on my lips then turned to Joe. "Just making arrangements with the love of my life, Joe." I could have actually killed her there and then.

"The love of your life? Gosh, I didn't realise you two were an item. Since when?"

"We've been together a couple of weeks now, haven't we?"

I looked at Joe and tried bloody hard to smile. "Yeah," I croaked.

"Anyway, I have to go, got class in a few minutes. See you later, big boy." Lisa blew me a kiss then glided from the room. I think I might have slunk to the floor.

Joe's eyes looked as though they were about to pop out of his head. "Fucking hell, you dark horse!" This was bound to be round the college by ten am.

"Look, Joe, I'd rather you didn't mention anything to anyone, not yet anyway."

"You and Lisa Hill? She's the catch of the college, mate. Good on ya, I say." He put his briefcase on the desk. "And why keep it a secret? You could do a lot worse than Lisa."

"She's just a bit...full on, like. Thinks we're properly together, like girlfriend and boyfriend together."

"And aren't you?"

"Well, I don't know her well enough yet. We've had two dates and I want to get to know her before we start going public."

"Reckon everyone'll know by the end of today, mate. Lisa isn't that good at keeping secrets."

"I've asked her not to say anything, not yet anyway."

"Well she's just told me." Joe laughed.

"Yeah, well, I guess she had to when you saw her bent over me."

"Arh, don't worry, your secret's safe with me. I'll be out of this place by the end of next week, I won't tell anyone. Though seriously, she's a nice girl, been around a bit I know, but she's clever and got great potential."

I nearly said she's not bad in bed either but decided not to put that thought in Joe's head as he did have a reputation with women.

At lunch time I decided to go to Jack's cafe and see Janice. Thoughts of Lisa and her undying love for me were starting to grate a little and I was a bit sick of Joe winking at me every five minutes and chuckling as he muttered under his breath 'won't be a secret much longer, ha-ha'. There were a couple of times I felt like throwing the stapler at him.

So there I was, on my way to Jack's cafe, excited at the thought of seeing Janice again. I could feel those butterflies in my stomach, though I wasn't sure if it was because I was worried about lying to Janice and Lisa, or if it was because I was genuinely looking forward to seeing Janice. I answered my own question when I approached the door. Janice was standing behind the counter, making a latte for someone when she looked up and saw me walk towards her. Her eyes seemed to light up and her whole body appeared to have a glow about it. I hadn't seen her for a few days, that last time being a fleeting visit with no time to chat. And here she was, pleased to see me and not seeming worried that we hadn't spent any real time together since our magical date the previous week.

"Hello, stranger," she said, the beautiful white teeth gleaming at me. "Haven't seen you in a while. I guess you've been busy with your new job."

I nodded. "I have. I'm getting hardly any time to myself at the moment but I'm learning what I need to."

"Go and sit down and I'll bring you something over. I've just made a batch of coronation chicken rolls." I smiled at her and turned to find a table. Billy Brown was cleaning the only one spare in the cafe, meaning I'd have to sit there.

He glared at me when I approached him. "You come in here to eat or just chat up the staff?"

"Well I haven't come in to chat you up, so don't look so worried," I laughed. I had hoped he'd laugh as well but he didn't.

"Why haven't you been in to see Janice all week?"

I sat down. "I've been busy. And what's it got to do with you anyway?"

"I don't want you using her. She told me about your night out and that you shagged her and I get the impression she's expecting it again. Thought you might have been eager but I reckon you've just used her for sex."

"I haven't used her at all. You've no need to worry about her. I appreciate why you do but you should stop being so protective. I'm sure Janice can stick up for herself." I wasn't too sure where I'd got this new-found confidence from but I liked it.

Billy glared at me, his eyes narrowed. "Just be warned," he said, before striding back to the counter.

Janice passed him on her way to my table. She put the roll and a mug of coffee in front of me and sat down. "I've got a few minutes," she said. "So, how have you been?"

"Good thanks. And you?" It was small talk, but it was better than nothing.

"I've missed you. Thought maybe we could have a get-together this week."

"Yeah, sorry about that. My mum's got a new man and he came for tea on Tuesday. It's been one of those weeks."

"What about this weekend, you doing anything?"

Looking at Janice's face I really didn't want to lie to her but I knew I'd have to. "I'm going to a stag do, it's all weekend I'm afraid so I won't be around." I took a bite of the roll and watched Janice's expression fall.

"Oh, that's a shame. I was going to ask if you wanted to come to my house as mum and dad are away Friday till Sunday."

I don't think it could have been worse timing. My face must have said it all, because Janice seemed to know what I was thinking even though I couldn't speak.

"It's okay, don't worry," she laughed. "There'll be other times before I emigrate. Maybe we can get together one night next week?"

Why couldn't life be this simple all the time? I thought. Trust me to have two girlfriends, keeping my options open, whilst one was a possessive sex maniac and the other was easy going and gentle. I half contemplated letting Lisa down gently but as I'd already tried that and failed miserably, I decided to just stick to my white lie.

"I'm really sorry, Janice. That would have been perfect as well. Do they go away often?"

"About every six weeks. Dad likes to keep an eye on the cafes he has in the south and he sometimes takes mum with him."

"Maybe we could get together next week then? How about Wednesday?"

"Wednesday sounds perfect. Do you want to ring me?"

"Yeah, I'll do that. Not sure when I'll be able to come back into the cafe as it's Joe's last week next week and I can't see that I'll be able to get away much."

I held Janice's hand for a moment and she leant over to kiss me before going back to the counter to a very angry-looking Billy Brown. She was so easy to get on with, so easy to have a relationship with. She wasn't interested in all that commitment and all the declaring of undying love bollocks. She just wanted to have a good time, no strings and no 'what time d'you call this' crap. I knew that if she wasn't moving to Australia I'd have been very close to telling Lisa the truth but I soon banished that thought on my way back to college as I saw her standing by her car, talking on her mobile phone.

I went over to her and tapped her on the arm. She turned around, tears in her eyes.

"What's up?" I asked when she hung up.

"You're going to hate me, Gary," she sobbed.

"Of course I'm not. What's happened?"

"I have to go to my parent's house this weekend. My dad isn't too well and my mum is a bit worried about him. She's asked if I can go on Friday after work. I said I'd got plans but I could tell she really wants me there."

"Of course you have to go," I said. "You must go. Your parents come first, always."

"Why don't you come with me?"

I spluttered. "No, I think it best you go alone, I'd only be in the way. I'll meet your parents another time, maybe when your dad's better."

"Are you sure? I feel terrible. You were so looking forward to this weekend as well. And I wanted to show you my new..." she lowered her voice, "lingerie. I bought it especially for you."

"Really, you go. You can show me next week when you get back."

She flung her arms around my neck and almost hugged the life out of me. "You're amazing, Gary. I love you, I really do." Kissing me in full view of the car park where windows were filled with guppy-fish faces, I knew Joe Mint had been right about our secret not being a secret for much longer.

I also knew I was a first class bastard as I couldn't wait to get home that night and ring Janice to tell her the good news. She picked up after about six rings and I thought for a moment she wasn't there and probably had a better offer. The thought of spending an entire weekend with her and that pert backside was turning me on no end.

"I hope you don't mind but I'm not going on the stag weekend now and so will be available if you still want me?"

Janice squealed. "Of course I do. Ooh, I'm so excited. Mum and dad will be going tomorrow afternoon so you can just come over after work if you like, but I'll leave it up to you. Come on Saturday if it suits you better."

"No, I'll come over tomorrow. It'll be about seven o'clock."

"Don't forget your overnight bag," she giggled.

"Did you want to go out anywhere?"

"I'm quite happy just staying in. I want you to take me from behind on Saturday afternoon in my front room."

I gasped and nearly dropped the phone. "Well, yeah, err, I will, of course I will."

She laughed. "I've always fantasised about having sex in our front room. Don't ask me why, it's just me being a bit of a pervert."

"You can be as much of a pervert as you like with me."

"Excellent, I'll get the bondage gear then."

That was going a bit too far.

Janice must have taken the phone away from her ear for a moment because I heard a lot of muffled laughter.

"You're so gullible. I was only joking. I'm not into bondage." She stopped laughing. "You're not into it are you?"

"God no, never been into all that kinky stuff."

"But you like my lacy undies though," she said, lowering her voice and purring down the phone line.

"Of course." I thought about Janice's lacy bra and the

way those amazing tits had poked from underneath it.

"So I'll see you tomorrow night then. Are you going to bring a takeaway or shall I cook something?"

"I'll bring a pizza if you like, and some wine."

"We have plenty of wine here. Dad has a well-stocked wine cellar. Just get a tasty pizza on your way."

I have to admit I'd been looking forward to a weekend with Lisa at her place, no doubt experimenting with different sexual positions in between cans of beer and Match of The Day. But after I'd made those arrangements with Janice I started to think it was her I was really fond of and Lisa was more of a sex conquest. To be honest, it wouldn't have bothered me if Janice and I didn't have sex over the weekend and we just spent time together. I wasn't sure if those feelings worried me or made me feel sorry for myself because after all, Janice would soon be gone and I'd either have to get used to a life of monogamy with Lisa or think very seriously about telling her the truth. Well, maybe not the truth, but at least finally letting her down gently.

I went out of my way to avoid her on Friday at work, knowing full well that I didn't want to have to lie to her face when she was upset about her dad being ill. I sent her a quick text mid-afternoon to say I hoped everything was okay and I was thinking about her. She shot me one back saying *'I love you; you're the best boyfriend a girl could have'*. God, I felt bad after reading that.

On my way home from work that afternoon I called in to see Alfie as he always finished early on Fridays, said it was a perk of being in a managerial position but I think he'd made the rule up so that he could get home early and start his weekend. He'd always been a lazy tosser, even at school. You'd often find him fast asleep in a broom cupboard or having a lie down in the nurse's office on the bed in there. He just didn't want to work, that was his problem. How the hell he'd landed the job as a manager was beyond me.

"I tell ya, man, sleep your way to the top, it always works," he'd said to me when I was going for the interview for the job at Dullsdale College.

"I will if I have to. But you're lucky, you never get caught. Knowing me, I'll get found out within my first day."

"You're crap at guilt, mate, that's your trouble. With all the birds you've had over the years you should be an expert at lying."

He was right; I should have been an expert. I was doing a pretty good job now wasn't I, even though I was feeling lousy about it. But I kept telling myself that within a couple of months Janice wouldn't be here anymore so wouldn't need to know any different. I could just enjoy some good times with her. And besides, I was pretty sure she felt the same. My suspicions were confirmed to me over the weekend.

Chapter Twelve

I arrived at Janice's house at seven on the dot, worried I might get the hands on hips stance I'd got from Lisa the other night when I turned up fifteen minutes late. I should have known better. Janice answered the door and ushered me inside, taking the pizza from my arms. I followed her into the kitchen where she started putting slices onto plates. I took the wine from the worktop and examined the label.

"Very nice," I said, reaching for the glasses she'd left out and pouring one each. We went back into the lounge and sat on the sofa side by side.

"I've been looking forward to this all day," she said, then leant over and kissed my cheek. "The pizza I mean," she laughed. "Though I have been looking forward to seeing you as well." She leant over and kissed my cheek again.

We carried on munching the pizza and sipping our wine. She'd put some music on in the background and it added to the atmosphere. I wouldn't have said it was romantic but it was definitely comfortable. I felt totally at ease with Janice sat in her front room on their sofa, stuffing my face with pizza. Thinking about it, I've never felt like that with anyone. It was like she knew my every thought, understood everything about me. She seemed to be in tune with my feelings, knowing that I didn't want to get married or make any heavy commitments but that I did feel close to her. I got the impression she felt exactly the same and I think that's what made me feel so at ease.

When the pizza was finished she took our plates into the kitchen whilst I refilled our glasses. She came back in with a box of chocolates and left them on the table.

"Those are for later," she said, then leant back and snuggled into me.

"What do you plan on doing with them?" I smirked.

"Eating them?" She hit my chest in a friendly gesture.

"Out of the box?" She sat up and looked at me, a smile dancing on her lips.

"I'll let you eat them off me if you like?"

"I'd like that very much." I was stuffed, filled with pizza and the thought of eating a caramel crème was making me heave, though the thought of eating Janice's nipples was seriously turning me on.

"Do you want to watch a film or something?" Janice stood up and went to the shelves that seemed to hold about a million DVD cases. "What d'you fancy?"

We chose a romantic film with Julia Roberts. It wasn't that good though I think we'd have switched it off sooner anyway because I could feel myself unable to wait much longer to see what delights Janice was hiding under the woolly jumper.

I pressed my lips hard against hers, stroking her face as I kissed her and she wrapped her arms around my neck, not making any moves towards my jeans but just happy to lay there and soak up the moment. I could hear people's voices coming from the television but I couldn't hear what they were saying; it didn't matter. The important thing was that I had Janice in my arms and we were entranced in a deep kiss, our tongues caressing each other's mouths as I continued to run my fingers around her face. Her skin was so smooth to touch, it felt like silk, and her lips seemed magnetically attached to mine.

My cock, firing on all cylinders now, must have nudged Janice as she suddenly moved her hand towards my jeans and unfastened the belt. I helped by unfastening the button and zip and releasing my impressive hard on. Janice went down on me, moving her whole body as she wrapped her mouth around my very erect companion. I'm surprised I didn't shoot the moment her tongue touched me because the way she was performing left no room for improvement. The tenderness as she moved her mouth up and down was sending shivers all around my body and I arched my back at one point, nearly choking the poor girl. But she continued to please me with her hand, lifting her face towards mine as she started kissing me again.

I put my hands up her jumper and slowly helped her remove it. Her white satin bra was the first thing I noticed, lace around the cups showing off her beautifully erect nipples. I pushed one of the cups to one side and moved in for the kill, my mouth taking hold of her breast as she carried on arousing me with her hand. I could still hear the film in the background, but there was nothing more than a blur now as Janice's moans swept through them and filled my head with thoughts of taking her from behind. I had a sudden urge to do just that and as I lifted myself from the sofa, she seemed to glide with me, manoeuvring herself for me to get a good grip. It was like I'd been reincarnated for good behaviour, only the person who'd reincarnated me wasn't the devil. Being inside Janice was everything I wanted it to be; it felt warm and comfortable. I was content, filled with thoughts of togetherness, and the word I dreaded to say to myself kept cropping up; love.

I wanted to just carry on shagging Janice from behind and stop the silly thoughts of making love to her; I didn't want those thoughts to interfere with the pleasure I was experiencing or the disappointment I would feel when she announced her imminent departure for the other side of the world. I didn't want to love Janice. It would be a nightmare. It was something I knew I couldn't experience, not with her, not now.

But I knew what we were doing was making love; we were totally comfortable with each other. This was different to how it had been with Lisa. We were two people who knew there was no pressure from either person, both not wanting to get in too deep. It could almost have been a 'friends with benefits' type of scenario, only I wasn't sure being friends with Janice was what I wanted anymore.

I reached a climax and took one last plunge before pulling out and letting Janice relax on the sofa. I sank to the floor, lifting my head to the ceiling as I closed my eyes and sighed with satisfaction. Janice did the same, lifting her legs up and wrapping them around my neck, her pussy now millimetres away from my mouth. I couldn't resist her and in I went, tongue sinking like it was going through quick sand. She was on fire and even though my flame was going out, I wasn't going to push her away just because I'd drooped.

"God, Gary, you are so good." I finished giving her oral sex and pulled away, wiping my mouth as I reached for my boxer shorts and put them on. "What am I going to do when I move away?" She laughed then and put her bra and knickers back on. I poured some more wine, waited for her to sit back down then handed her a glass.

"Are you definitely going?" I asked, a part of me hoping she'd changed her mind, perhaps even since she'd met me.

"Yes, in two months. I've got enough money saved up now and I'm just waiting for the flat I've rented to be vacated by the current tenants.

"So we've got two months together then?"

She laughed again. I was starting to get a complex. "I'm afraid so. Though I've got tons to do before I go so this might be one of the few weekends we'll get to spend together. You're not upset about me going are you?"

"Gosh no," I lied. "I'm happy for you. Just a shame we've only just met really." I clinked my glass against hers. "Here's to you and hoping you'll be very happy with your new life in Oz."

"Thanks, I appreciate that. It's so good to know that I've finally found someone who won't stand in my way and make me feel guilty for leaving. I wish we'd got together sooner but it's typical isn't it. Oh well, let's just enjoy the time we have left."

"I'll drink to that," I said, taking a large gulp and hoping Janice hadn't noticed the disappointment in my voice.

"I'm quite looking forward to meeting new people, finding new friends. I'll have to find a new 'friend with benefits' of course, but I'm sure I will."

I looked at her. "Friend with benefits?" I asked.

"Yeah, you know, a boyfriend that isn't interested in commitment or getting heavy, someone I can sleep with every now and then, have a good time with, and not get bogged down with all that falling in love bollocks." She snuggled closer into me. "Someone like you really."

I had a nervous habit where I scratched my nose when I wasn't sure what to say next. Right then I was going for a world record of nose scratching.

"Oh right, yeah, I see what you mean." Did I? I thought. "Well, you're bound to find someone, a gorgeous girl like you. But don't you want to fall in love one day?"

"Well, maybe one day. But I'm only twenty-four, I've

got my whole life ahead of me." She had a point. I was only twenty-seven and I thought the same. "You don't want to fall in love yet do you?"

I scoffed and took a gulp of wine. "God no, never. I mean, far too young for all that shit. Nah, I like nights out with the lads and adding notches to my bedpost."

"Well, I'm not sure about notches, haven't got many of those, but I like to enjoy life, like we're doing now."

The word 'love' seemed to make its way up my throat and I quickly gulped it down. Either I'd misread Janice's flirtatious moves on me in Jack's cafe or I was a complete dick head. Actually, I kind of thought both seemed most likely. I looked at the box of chocolates still on the table.

"Anyway, aren't you going to open those chocolates?" I asked.

Janice picked up the box and opened it. She took one out and placed it on her breast. "There you go. All yours." I lifted it off with my mouth and felt its creamy centre slide down my throat. "And another one." She picked another chocolate from the box and placed it on the other breast from where I duly took it in the same way, this time not feeling any arousal. I wondered if the conversation about being friends with benefits had turned me off in some way though I have to admit it was easier to not get too involved when I knew she wouldn't be around in two months. Having a 'friend with benefits' would, in any other circumstances, be my dream come true, but it just didn't feel that way with Janice. I really liked her and didn't want to think we were just meeting for a quickie every now and then, only to say goodbye one day and never grace each other's presence again. It all seemed wrong somehow.

We spent most of Saturday morning in bed, wrapped around each other, enjoying the warmth of each other's bodies. To be honest, I could have stayed there all day but the fact that Janice saw me more as a friend than a boy-friend was niggling at the back of my mind. I felt I might need to distance myself, sooner rather than later, and so I started to think about Lisa and how she'd be getting on with her parents. She hadn't told me much about them though I got the impression she was close to them, especially having gone to spend the weekend with her poorly dad. I turned over in the bed and looked at my mobile phone. After turning back to look at Janice I got out of bed, grabbed the phone and crept downstairs. When I got to the front room I switched the phone on, pressing it against my chest to dull the noise as it sprung into life. Then I dialled Lisa's number.

"Gary," she said in a happy tone, obviously pleased that I'd rung.

"Hi, I hope it's okay to ring while you're at your parents' house?"

"Of course it is. I've really missed you. I rang you last night but it went straight through to voice mail."

My first thought was 'phew, thank God I turned my phone off as soon as I got to Janice's house.'

"Oh, sorry about that, my battery's been dead, just charged it up now." Always a good excuse. "How are you, how's your dad?"

"I'm okay, though would have been better if you'd been here. My dad's struggling. Think mum's really worried about him."

"What's wrong with him?" I moved into the kitchen, holding the phone against my ear with my shoulder as I filled the kettle.

"He has flu. Mum just said it was man-flu at first but he hasn't got any better so the doctor's put him on antibiotics. He'll be okay I'm sure."

"Of course he will. Us men make terrible patients, especially when we've got man-flu." I laughed, reaching for a mug.

"Where are you?"

"At home," I lied.

"Shall I ring you on your landline? My mum has one of those free-calls-at-weekends offers."

"No, I've got tons of minutes left on this. Anyway, haven't got long." I thought I heard movement upstairs and went to close the kitchen door. "I've missed you," I said, though wasn't sure if I really had missed her. It just seemed like the best thing to say at the time.

"Can't you come down today? My mum will be ever so pleased to meet you and it might cheer dad up as well."

There was definitely movement upstairs and I heard footsteps on the landing, making their way to the top of the stairs. "I'm sorry, I can't come today, got such a lot to do." I hesitated. "Oh bugger, there's someone at the door, got to go, sweetheart."

"Will you ring me later?"

"Yeah, I'll ring you tonight. Say hi to your folks for me." I hung up just as Janice walked through the door. She was wearing a cotton shirt and I could just see a pair of pink knickers poking from underneath it.

"Who are you talking to?" she asked, going over to the kettle.

"Alfie." The lies were fast and furious and I felt I needed to get a grip.

"Do you want some breakfast?"

I looked at my watch. "It's nearly midday."

"Lunch then. How about beans on toast? Or a fry up?"

"A fry up sounds good to me. Mind if I have a quick shower?"

"No, go ahead. I'll get lunch sorted then we can have a think about what we want to do this afternoon."

I tapped her arse as I walked past, making my way to the kitchen door. I decided to turn my phone off and put it in my bag. The last thing I wanted was for Janice to know I'd lied to her, especially when it was really Janice I wanted to be with.

We watched a couple of films that afternoon, snuggled up on the sofa eating the rest of the chocolates, a bowl of popcorn on the table. It all felt so easy, so comforting. Being with Janice could have been the making of me if I hadn't had thoughts of Lisa riding through my head at a hundred miles an hour. I wasn't sure I wanted to stay at Janice's that night and sat in the bathroom for fifteen minutes worrying about what I was getting myself into. I really needed to distance myself from our 'friendship' and either concentrate more on Lisa or just tell Janice I didn't think it was going to work out. Either way, I was in a right dilemma and it was driving me nuts.

At six o'clock I suggested going out for a takeaway, mainly so I could ring Lisa as I'd promised. But then Janice asked me to sit down saying she thought we should talk. I sat in the armchair and watched as she tucked her legs underneath herself on the sofa opposite. I could sense a slightly uncomfortable feeling in the air and couldn't help but feel a bit sad that something was up, especially after the cosy afternoon we'd had and the very passionate Friday night in.

"Don't you want a takeaway?" I asked, wondering if she wanted to go out to a restaurant.

"The thing is, Gary, I'm getting the impression you're seeing our friendship as something more and I just need to make you understand that I can't get too involved with you. I'm so sorry if I've misled you."

I stared at her, convinced she was psychic. "No, of course not. I listened to what you said last night and that's fine by me."

"It's just that, well, I really like you, like *really* like you, and I'm worried that when the time comes for me to move it's going to be really tough for both of us."

I needed to man up. I'd obviously given her the impression that I was utterly smitten, which of course I was, but I had an image to maintain. I'd never given a girl that impression before, but I'd never met a girl like Janice until now.

"You have nothing to worry about. For the record, I really like you, too. But when the time comes for you to move to Oz, we'll just say our goodbyes and move on. You'll have guys clamouring after you over there; those Ozzies are a bunch of randy sods you know, you won't stand a chance." I laughed. She laughed with me. Though I felt it was a bit false.

"Thanks, Gary," she said, a slightly relieved look appearing on her face. "I just don't want to get serious and then find I can't move. I've been planning this for a long time and everything's been arranged, plus I have a cafe to open once I'm settled over there."

I went over and sat next to her on the sofa. "Stop worrying. We don't need to spend too much time together, just the occasional night or whatever." I cupped her face in my hands and gently kissed her lips. "Look, I'm going to go home tonight and leave you on your own. I think it's probably for the best."

Much to my dismay, she nodded and smiled. "I knew you'd understand. You're a very special person and one day you'll make someone an amazing husband. You really don't need to go though, we can still enjoy tonight."

"No, I think it's best." I stood up and went to the door. "We've had a lovely time so let's not spoil it by talking about what could have been."

Part of me felt like this was goodbye. I had a feeling that once I'd walked out of that door, Janice would forget about me and lunch at Jack's cafe would go back to being just that, lunch.

As I drove home I thought about how much I'd enjoyed spending time with Janice and how amazing a relationship with her could have been. It really was a shame that she was moving away but it was just bad timing. If I'd asked her out before I did maybe things would have been different. She was right, it wasn't a good idea that we got too involved for fear of making that last goodbye a painful one, and I think that's why I respected her so much. She wasn't willing to just jump into a relationship with someone knowing full well that she'd have to end it before long. She cared about people, and it was obvious she cared about me. It made it all the more difficult of course but I was a grown man, I'd learn to live with the fact I'd been more or less dumped by the one woman I was genuinely fond of.

Chapter Thirteen

I got home to lights on upstairs but none downstairs, and Terry's Mercedes parked in the drive. Great, I thought, just what I need. I quietly put the key in the lock and turned the handle then stepped into the hall only to hear my mum shouting upstairs what sounded like 'harder, Terry, harder'. I was more than embarrassed. My mother was shagging. How could that be, my own mother, having sex upstairs with her toy boy? I hovered about in the hall for a few minutes wondering whether I should go back out. The thought of sleeping in the next room to my mum and Terry was sending shivers down my spine, and not in a good way. Mums don't have sex, I thought, as I put my bag on the floor. Not *my* mum anyway.

It was all too much and I picked the bag up again then left the house, softly closing the front door so as not to disturb the noisy events upstairs. Part of me wished I'd stayed at Janice's after all, at least I could have had a shag as well. The thought of me now being on my own whilst my own mother was having it away with a guy more than a decade younger than her made me feel queasy. I got in the car and turned over the engine then set off down the road. The only place I could think of going was Alfie's. At least Jez would probably be there as well. It was still early so I assumed they'd be in.

I was lucky, they were at Alfie's planning their night on the town when I arrived. Both dressed to the nines they laughed when they saw me and I knew I'd have to tell more lies just to stop myself looking like a right tit.

"Throw you out did she?" Alfie laughed.

"Don't be daft," I mocked. "Nah, fancied a night out with you numpties. She was a bit full on."

Alfie looked at Jez. "Thought you were spending all weekend there, shagging for England, while your other bit's away. Come on, Gaz, spill."

"There's nothing to spill. We had a good night last night, if you know what I mean." I winked. "And today we've had a nice time but I don't want to get in too deep. She's good company. Just a friend with benefits."

"Friend with benefits? Bloody hell, Gaz, how many of them have you had now? Every one of your girlfriends seems to be a friend with benefits. I tell you, mate, you need admitting for addiction. You should take a leaf out of my book once in a while." Jez surprised me when he said that, so much so, even Alfie looked his way.

"Have you been on the loopy juice, Jez?" Alfie asked.

"Not yet, but I do have an announcement to make. And you'd better not piss your sides laughing."

We both glared at Jez.

"I've been seeing a girl from work and I think it might be a bit serious."

My first thought was of Julie, Izzy and Cath, the three girls Jez and Alfie had enjoyed an orgy with the other week. "What do you mean, serious?" I asked.

"Well, you know, like we're getting quite close. She knows about my past and isn't bothered. Says she doesn't want to talk about what I got up to before we got together and is just interested in getting to know me now. In fact, she'll be in the Horse Shoe tonight so I thought I might introduce you to her."

Jez was the last person I expected to get serious with a girl. The way he ogled my mum, the flirting and the frivolity with anything in a skirt didn't put him in the bracket of 'settling down type'. But maybe we were seeing a different side to him. It's amazing what a nice girl could do, though I decided to reserve judgement on the 'nice' until I'd seen her.

"So what's her name?" Alfie asked.

"Angela Jones. She's tall, blonde, shapely, just my type really. She's also a really nice girl and I don't want you two showing me up."

"Think you do a good enough job of that yourself, mate," I laughed, thumping Jez on the arm. "Don't worry, we'll be on our best behaviour. I'm happy for you actually. Think it's nice that you've found yourself a decent woman for a change."

"What about you," Alfie asked me, "and that Lisa bird?"

Shit, I'd forgotten to ring Lisa. I'd promised her I'd ring at six o'clock and had completely forgotten after leaving Janice's house. I fumbled about in my bag for my phone and switched it on. There were five text messages from Lisa and two missed calls.

"Hi Gary," the first call said, "sorry I missed you. I'll try again later. I imagine you're having your tea. Bye."

The second one said, "Thought you were going to ring me. It's quarter to seven. I'm in all night. Bye for now."

It was the text messages that made me cringe when Lisa ended her first message with "luv u x" and her last message with "thought we had something special, guess I was wrong."

I hit the key to dial her number, ignoring Alfie as he sniggered next to me. He really needed to grow up.

"Lisa," I said, when she finally picked up. "I'm so sorry, honey. Got carried away with reading and then I had my tea and have only just realised what time it is. I left my phone switched off."

"Have I done something to upset you?" came the irritable reply.

"Of course not, it's my fault. I'm so sorry. Will you forgive me?" Alfie had to move away for fear of falling over in hysterics. Jez just went into the lounge and sat down.

"Yes, I forgive you, but you've got some making up to do next week. I thought you'd dumped me and I'm upset enough this weekend as it is."

"Is your dad feeling better?" Changing the subject was always a good move.

"He's a bit better thanks, seems to have perked up. Mum reckons he was putting it on after all and it was just man-flu."

I thought I should defend Lisa's dad, being a sufferer of man-flu myself a few times. "Or it could be that the antibiotics are working?"

"Well, yes, that's probably true, though I can't wait to go home tomorrow. Mum's driving me mad. She's insisting on meeting you. Said she was really disappointed you didn't come with me this weekend and asked if we're just friends." Lisa paused while I composed myself and watched Alfie stumble into the lounge, still sniggering, to join Jez. "Are we just friends, Gary?"

I honestly wasn't sure how to answer that. But I put her mind at rest anyway. "Friends?" I said, trying to get my voice to show surprise. "I'd like to think we're more than friends now."

She sighed. "Oh, I'm so glad you think that. I feel we're going to be really good together. Mum says she and dad will come to stay with me when he's feeling back to normal and then you can come for dinner and meet them. They're going to love you, I just know it."

I wondered what exactly Lisa had told them about me. "Yeah, sounds good." Alfie was pointing to the clock on the mantel piece. "Anyway, I hope you don't mind but I'm at Alfie's place and we're just going out for a curry. Shall I ring you later?"

"I wish we were going out for a curry. I can't tell you how much I'm missing you. Just hearing your voice is giving me an orgasm." Nice, I thought, girls had commented on my voice before but I don't remember any of them saying it'd given them an orgasm. "Ring me when you get home will you? It doesn't matter what time it is. I'll keep my mobile switched on and will be waiting for your call." She hesitated. "And Gary?"

"Yes," I said, a little caution in my voice now.

"Let me leave you with this thought; I'm currently wearing absolutely nothing and my hands are stroking a place that your tongue loves to explore." It was then that my cock jumped to attention and I had to walk away from Alfie's lounge door and make my way to the bathroom where I tried to soften the hard on that was becoming more prominent with every breath.

"That thought will stay with me all night," I said, adjusting myself and hoping Alfie and Jez didn't see what Lisa's words had just done.

"Bye, honey-bun," she purred, then hung up.

Alfie and Jez gave me a look when I went into the lounge to join them as though to say 'what the fuck?' I wasn't going to indulge them in Lisa's nakedness so I shrugged and asked if they were ready to go.

We met Angela in the Horse Shoe at nine o'clock. Jez seemed quite taken with her as he put his arm around her waist and kissed her, in full view of Alfie and me. It was something we weren't used to, seeing Jez being amorous, but I have to admit, him and Angela looked good together. I took to her straight away; her long slim legs and sleek golden locks probably did it initially but she really did seem like a nice person, not at all like the munters Jez usually went for. I actually thought he might have cracked it this time.

It turned out Angela knew Lisa quite well as they went to college together. I wasn't going to mention Lisa but Jez brought the subject up and I couldn't get out of it. I was just glad Alfie didn't mention Janice or I could have come across as being a right dick.

"Lisa's a lovely girl," Angela said. "She was a very loyal friend to me at college. We lost touch after a few months and she went on to get herself the job at Dullsdale. It's brilliant that she's still there."

"She's done well for herself," I pointed out, noticing Alfie's raised eyebrows. "What? She's a great girl."

"I've already told you, mate, been around the block a few times."

"Well even if she has, she's a nice girl and we get on grand. I'm not interested in what she used to get up to."

"Absolutely, I couldn't agree more." Angela looked up into Jez's eyes. "I've already said to Jeremy, what he did in his past is none of my business, it's what's happening now that's important." Jeremy? He was well under the thumb.

Alfie sniggered when Angela had used Jez's official name, it was a name he'd told us never to call him. He blushed bright red and gulped back his pint, firming his grip on Angela's waist.

"Where are you heading off to next?" he asked Angela.

"Thought we might go to Banana's for a bit. There's a band on tonight and it sounds quite good. They played at Monday's the other night and got really good reviews. Fancy joining us?" Angela reached up and kissed Jez on the cheek.

"I'd love to but I'd better ask the others." He turned to Alfie and me and we both shrugged in unison.

"Fine by me," Alfie said. "I hear there's some talent

goes in there."

"Yeah, I'm up for it," I agreed, knocking back my pint and putting the empty glass on the bar.

"I'll just go and tell the others you'll be joining us. They'll be made up." Angela tottered off towards the corner of the pub where a group of very attractive girls stood, holding drinks and chatting. Within minutes she tottered back, her high heels clattering on the stone flags.

"Mandy and Shell are coming but the others aren't bothered. Is that okay?"

"As long as I'm with you that's absolutely fine," Jez said, as Alfie stuck his fingers in his mouth and pretended to barf.

Angela's friends came towards us, their eyes flicking from me to Alfie as though they were weighing up which one of us to go for. It was quite unnerving for me as I was already up to my neck in it having Janice and Lisa on the go, so the last thing I needed was someone else to complicate things. Alfie was in his element though, as he went towards them both, stood in between them and put his arms around their shoulders. The six of us then left the pub and made our way to Banana's night club, a posh place just up the road where quite a lot of footballers and wannabe WAGs hung out. It was a place I would have taken Janice if she'd have stayed around and we'd become a proper item, and come to think of it once she was out of the country, I wondered if it was somewhere Lisa would want to go. Most probably, I thought, as I watched Alfie open the double doors and gently guide his little harem into the building. Jez and Angela were walking hand in hand whilst I was bringing up the rear, a part of me wondering whether I should just go home and leave them to it.

The music was thumping inside and a DJ stood on a platform in the middle of the dance floor, mumbling into a microphone as bodies flung themselves around the wooden flooring and bar staff ran from one end of the bar to the other, desperate for a decent tip. It was my round and I got the girls' orders before going to the bar. The barman put the drinks on a tray and I handed him the money, telling him to keep the change. The round came to just short of thirty-quid; I wouldn't be getting another, that was for sure.

I turned around and started walking back to the table where the others were sat, Alfie in between Mandy and Shell whilst Jez and Angela were kissing in the corner.

"Gary?"

I turned my head in the direction of my name being called. And there she stood, up rather close to a big guy, dressed to kill and looking every bit the wannabe WAG as I'd ever seen. I smiled and probably looked quite shocked, rooted to the spot as she started to walk towards me, the big guy striding behind.

"Hey, what are you doing here?" Janice looked at me as though she'd just seen a long lost friend.

"Janice, hi, err, I didn't realise you were coming in here tonight." As my hands started shaking I heard the glasses start to rattle.

"Yeah, after you left I got bored so thought I'd come here and see who was about. I come in here a lot. I take it you're with someone?" She looked at the tray of drinks that now rested precariously in my hands.

"Alfie and Jez, oh, and their girlfriends. I did go home but mum was there with her boyfriend so thought I'd see what the lads were doing instead."

"Oh, right. Hope you were okay about before?"

I looked at the big guy who was now eyeing me up suspiciously.

"Sorry," Janice turned to him. "Paul, this is Gary." He held out his hand then reeled it back in when he realised I didn't have a spare hand to shake.

"Good to meet you," he boomed.

"Yeah, likewise." I looked down at the drinks. "I need to get these to the table. I'll see you soon." I looked into Janice's eyes and could have sworn I saw a look of embarrassment.

"Probably see you next week at the cafe then?" Janice shouted after me as I started to walk away. I nodded, unable to turn around again for fear of Janice seeing the confusion on my face.

When I got back to the table you'd think Alfie had become Hugh Hefner as he handed a glass of wine to each of his new girlfriends. I took my bottle of lager and wrapped my mouth around the rim, gulping it back, wondering what the hell I'd just walked into. What was Janice playing at? Who the hell was Paul? I knew she just saw me as a 'friend with benefits' but to rub my face in it was just plain cruel. I knew Alfie would spend the night taking the piss out of me if I stayed because the look on my face would have told him instantly that something had got to me, so I downed the lager then stood up.

"Look, guys, I'm really not feeling too good so I'm going to make a move." Jez managed to prize his lips away from Angela's and looked at me. "Sorry, but my head's thumping.

"No worries, mate," Jez said. "Speak to you next week." And with that he turned back to Angela and carried on eating her.

Mandy and Shell didn't look one bit disappointed to see me leave which meant Alfie was most likely to get the cream. I almost ran out the door, down the street towards the taxi rank where I climbed into a black cab and asked the driver to take me home. Fortunately, I'd chosen a cab with a miserable driver who had no intention of conversing with me which meant I could think throughout the twenty minute ride back to my house in silence with just my confused thoughts to keep me company.

I was glad to see that Terry's car had gone when I

got home, though I could have done with him being there to give me a lift to Alfie's to collect my car. I opened the front door, poured myself a glass of water then went to my room. My weekend of passion with Janice had not gone to plan and as I lay on my bed looking at the ceiling thinking how much of a cock up I was making of my life, I started to think about Lisa. I switched my phone on and dialled her number. It was only half-past ten so I knew she'd still be up. She was, and answered after two rings. I can honestly say I'd never been as pleased to hear her voice. It was like nectar and it was then that I realised Lisa was probably the best thing that had happened to me for a long time. Wasting my time on Janice, a girl who just wanted a quick shag every now and then, just to get her through the next few months before she emigrated, wasn't what I wanted at all. Lisa's full-on approach to our relationship wasn't exactly what I wanted either but comparing them both, Lisa obviously thought a lot more about me than Janice ever would. My mind was made up. I wouldn't see Janice anymore and would concentrate my time on Lisa, see if we could make a go of our relationship and maybe one day she could introduce me to her parents. After all, she'd already met my mum, perhaps under false pretences, but mum was cool with it and so I knew it wouldn't be awkward to bring her back here again soon.

"Hi, darling," Lisa said, when she answered her mobile phone. "Thought you were going for a curry with your mates?"

"I was, but we ended up just having a few drinks. Anyway, I couldn't wait to talk to you so I came home." That would surely earn me a few Brownie points.

"Oh, you're such a sweetie." Result. "I so need to see you tomorrow night when I get home. Will you come over?"

"I'll come about seven-ish but I won't stay overnight, if you don't mind."

"No, of course not. Just five minutes will be enough," she purred. "Though I don't think five minutes will be enough to show you my new purchase."

"Which is?"

"You'll have to wait and see," she teased.

"Are you naked?" I had it bad.

"Ha-ha, no, not right now, sweetie. I'm fully clothed in pyjamas, though I am on my own in my old bedroom. Would you like me to be naked?"

We spent the rest of the call having phone- sex. She was an expert at it, knew all the things to say at the right times, and at the end of it she took a photo of herself in all her glory and texted it to me. Full on or not, this was one hot lady and I knew if I didn't pursue what seemed to be quickly developing, I'd be losing a very good thing.

Chapter Fourteen

I could tell mum had had a good night when I found her sat at the kitchen table the following morning reading the newspaper's supplement magazine. She looked up at me and grinned.

"There's coffee in the pot, son. Did you enjoy your weekend?"

I was too knackered to give mum the lowdown on Janice making me feel like a dick and Lisa saying she loved me, so I poured myself a coffee, grabbed a handful of biscuits, shrugged and left the room.

"That good, eh? I don't know, Gary, you'll be thirty in a couple of years. Don't you think it's time you started thinking about settling down?"

I turned back to look at mum. "I'm going back to bed," I mumbled. She said something else but I didn't quite catch it, though it sounded like 'what a cock'.

When I got back to my room I lay on the bed and switched my phone on to see a dozen text messages from Lisa, most of them telling me how much she loved me and one saying she couldn't wait to see me later.

Thoughts of Janice were racing through my head as I thought about her standing with the big guy, looking at me as though I was just a mate she hadn't seen for ages, not a guy she was supposed to fancy like mad who'd recently spent a fortune on her at one of the most expensive restaurants in Bedworth, only to shag her senseless and enjoy twenty-four hours of pure ecstasy with. Maybe she did that with all the guys, I thought, sipping my coffee and feeling like shit.

The day went by with more text messages from Lisa and a phone call when she'd arrived home. Her mum had made a beef casserole for us so she rang to make sure I didn't eat before I went round. Then she purred down the phone and told me not to be late. I made sure mum knew not to make me anything for tea before I walked over to Alfie's apartment block to collect my car and drive to Lisa's. I'd splashed out on a bottle of Cava though I didn't intend having much of it due to needing to drive home again.

Lisa opened the door as I was getting out of the car. I wasn't sure if her keenness was a little off-putting or whether it excited me but as I strode towards her she held out her arms then flung them around my neck, kissing me hard on the lips. We went inside and she kicked the door shut, still holding onto my neck. I put the bottle of Cava on the telephone table and put my arms around her waist, rubbing my hands up and down her back, soaking up her kisses and feeling completely needed. I knew I was onto a good thing when she slipped her hand down my pants.

"Let's open the champagne," I suggested, gently pulling away, wanting to contain my excitement for after I'd eaten. Truth is I was starving. Mum had offered to make me a mid-afternoon snack but I'd refused having noticed a bit of a bulge going on around my middle. I was worried I might have been indulging on too many takeaways and cans of beer, none of which were doing my waistline any good. But now I needed food and right then it was the only thing on my menu.

Lisa held my hand and led me into the kitchen where she'd laid the table with wine glasses and cutlery. A large brown pot sat on the hob and she stirred the contents with the wooden spoon that rested in it. It smelt delicious and made my stomach growl. She passed me the corkscrew and I opened the Cava, pouring some into two glasses.

"Now, sit down and I'll serve. This is mum's speciality; she's an expert at making casseroles."

The saying 'look at the mother and that's what the daughter will turn out like' was running through my thoughts as I took the first mouthful of casserole, realising that if Lisa could cook like this she'd definitely do for me. We sat looking into each other's eyes, clinking glasses and taking tiny mouthfuls of casserole. It was all very romantic and not at all like I was used to. But it was also very pleasant, and for the first time I actually felt comfortable as Lisa looked at me lovingly. Her light brown hair fell loosely against her shoulders and at one point I moved a few strands away from her face. Despite the fact I'd been thinking about Janice most of the day and the fact I shouldn't have been doing, Lisa was quickly growing on me and I could sense myself becoming smitten.

Dessert was raspberry pavlova, one of my favourites, though shop bought ones never matched up to the ones my mum made. Lisa put some cream on her finger and placed it in my mouth. I licked the tip of her finger then stroked her hand.

"Do you want some coffee?" she asked.

"Not right now," I said, watching her lips move as she folded her arms and rested them on the table, her breasts pushing out the top of her blouse.

I was too full to acknowledge the stirring in my pants but I suggested we sat on the sofa for half an hour, let our food go down, and then have a coffee and perhaps whatever popped up next. She giggled as she stood up, taking the plates into the kitchen.

"Go and sit down then, I'll be with you in a minute."

I could hear her humming in the kitchen and as I sank into the sofa, leaning back and closing my eyes, I'd never felt as content as I felt right there and then. Maybe I was under Lisa's spell at last, she'd reeled me in and caught me hook, line and sinker, and to be honest I loved every minute of it. Lisa wanted and needed me. She wasn't just with me for sex which was what most of my other girlfriends had been with me for; though to be fair, that was the case both ways. I knew I didn't have a future with Janice and after seeing her with the big guy I had to make myself stop thinking about her. She was just a girl I'd met in the cafe in the precinct. We'd had a date, found we were good in bed together then we'd gone our separate ways. There was no point dwelling on what could have been, or the what ifs about something that would never have worked. Lisa joined me in the lounge and snuggled into me on the sofa, resting her head against my chest and lifting her legs up underneath her. Enya was playing in the background adding to the atmosphere and the relaxing tone of the evening. I lifted her face to meet mine then kissed her.

"Thank you for a lovely meal," I said, smiling into her beautiful eyes.

"My mum made it, but you're very welcome. I hope there'll be many more." I think it was a question though she snuggled herself back into me again so I wasn't sure I should answer. I liked the idea of there being many more and tightened my grip on her, closing my eyes and taking in the sweet scent of her perfume.

"I'm glad your dad's feeling better. I think girls are closer to their dads aren't they?"

"I've always been close to my dad," she answered, shuffling away so we were sat side by side. She took hold of my hand and stroked it. "I'd love to give him a grandchild one day." I looked down at her. "Don't worry," she smiled, "I'm not asking to have a baby with you. It's just something I'd like one day, maybe when I'm in my 30s."

I have to say part of me was relieved, but another part of me felt a bit strange, a feeling I'd never experienced, as though I was levitating above myself and looking down on my twin in a parallel universe.

"I'd like kids one day," I said. "I want to be settled first though. It's a big responsibility isn't it?"

"I imagine so. My friend has two boys and she's often at her wit's end. But she chose to have kids, they weren't an accident or anything, so I never have much sympathy for her when she rings to tell me of Aaron's latest disaster or Daniel's recent mishap. I'd love to be a mum but I wouldn't want to become one of those stay at home mums who spends all her time bitching about school gate mums and the price of rubber gloves. Thing is, I also love my job and don't really want to give it up, so whoever I have kids with will need to be very understanding."

"I'm sure they will be." I hoped her comment about whoever she had kids with was a bit of a throw-away remark because I was finally getting used to being in a relationship with her and couldn't bear the thought of her turning out to be another Janice.

"Gary?" Lisa looked into my eyes.

"Yes."

"I know it's really early days and we're both still getting to know each other, but if we did stay together and things worked out for us in the future, do you reckon we'd have kids one day?"

I kissed her gently on the mouth. She looked so innocent and angelic, like a different Lisa to the one I knew at college who strode up and down the corridors, cleavage on show, arse wiggling, asserting her authority at spotty eighteen year olds with too much testosterone.

"I imagine so," I replied. She reached up and kissed me, pressing her lips against mine with impatience.

"I know you're not ready to say it back to me Gary, but I love you. I've had a lot of boyfriends over the last few years and I know I've got myself a bit of a reputation for being an 'easy ride'. But I've changed. You've changed me. You've made me see that I want you, more than I've ever wanted anyone."

Listening to her recite those words reminded me of myself. It was starting to click that Lisa and I were very similar. I lifted her face up to mine and kissed her softly before pulling away and looking deep into her eyes.

"I love you."

I wasn't sure where the words came from. It was an out-of-body experience. I'd never told a girl I loved her before, and even though I'd come close to telling Janice recently only to be relieved that I hadn't after I'd seen her with the big guy, I realised that saying those three little words was something that hadn't come easy to me. I wouldn't have said it if I didn't mean it. That much I knew for sure. Lisa stared at me, her eyes glinting and her cherry lips puckered ready to go in for the kill. Being Lisa's boyfriend and potential future wasn't so bad after all.

Suffice to say, we didn't bother with coffee that night.

Chapter Fifteen

Seeing Lisa's smiling face at work that following day was making me weak at the knees. Even Joe noticed I'd got it bad and apart from trying his best to take the piss, he kept whistling the theme tune to Love Story. When Lisa knocked on the office door and walked in I thought he was going to have a fit as he shot out of his chair and said "I'll leave you two love birds to it." Lisa grinned and came over to me.

"Have you been talking to Joe about us?"

"Yeah, I might have mentioned it," I said, grinning back.

"Just wondered how you are after last night?"

The love making had been phenomenal. I made the point of really getting to know every part of Lisa as she lay back on the bed and left me to explore her body. Not one thought of Janice or any other girl had gone through my mind and Lisa had completely taken me over. I was a man on a mission, someone different to the Gary Stringer I was used to. But I liked this new me. I was actually looking forward to introducing him to Jez and

Alfie, though Jez already seemed smitten and would understand perfectly. I felt a bit sorry for Alfie though, wondering if he'd ever find someone to settle down with, wondering whether he really wanted to, which I suspected he didn't.

"You sent me to heaven and back last night, how do you think I am?" I laughed.

"I'm free every night this week, no meetings or gym classes. The instructor's gone on holiday so I thought I'd give myself a week off. You're welcome to come and stay if you like?"

I pondered that thought. It would have been nice but I really wanted to get settled in my new job before I started staying over at Lisa's during the week. I needed to apply full concentration and I knew having her cleavage thrust in my face every morning before work would definitely scupper my 'getting on with the job' plans.

"I'll come over tomorrow night, but I won't stay. I'll get us a Chinese."

"We could go out?"

"Where do you fancy going?"

"Pictures? A restaurant? I don't mind. If you'd rather stay in though, I'm easy."

I grabbed her hand and pulled her towards me. "You sure were easy last night." She bent down and I put my hand on the back of her head then kissed her.

"You do strange things to me. I've never known anyone like you before." She drew away from me and stood at the other side of the desk, applying a more professional expression. "Right, if I don't see you before, I'll see you tomorrow night. Bring a Chinese with you and we'll carry on getting to know each other. We can do the pictures at the weekend perhaps."

"Sounds like a plan," I smiled, as Joe reappeared in the doorway.

"You two finished?" he said, grinning inanely at me.

"For now," I chuckled as I watched Lisa glide from my new office and into the corridor.

"Got yourself a right goer there, mate." Joe sat down at the other desk and started shuffling papers.

"So you keep telling me," I mused. "We're actually getting quite serious. I have a feeling Lisa's 'easy ride' days are well and truly behind her."

"Sounds like *you've* been behind her, eh?" He laughed loudly. "And what about *your* easy ride days, are they behind *you*?" he asked, still grinning.

"I reckon so."

"Fucking hell, you *have* got it bad. Well, I hope it works out for you, I really do. You make a nice couple and Lisa's a decent girl, hard working too. You could do a lot worse." And with that, he picked up a file and wheeled his chair over to my desk. "Right, better crack on, mate. Got work to do."

I stayed away from Jack's cafe for the next few weeks, mainly to avoid Janice. But I wasn't sure I wanted a run in with Billy Brown and him getting the wrong impression that I'd dumped Janice or something. I had thought about her, probably more than I should if truth be known, especially as Lisa and I were getting serious and the word 'love' was cropping up more and more, on a daily basis. But Janice had my phone number and I assumed if she really wondered where I was, or if she wanted to see me, she'd have rung. She didn't ring so I decided to move on. I'd even got into the habit of making sandwiches every day just so I could sit in Lisa's classroom and eat them with her. Of course, it wasn't every day we could spend our lunch breaks together as she often had a meeting to attend or I had a student to help. But the days we did spend together were getting very special and I found myself whistling each time I was buttering bread and slicing the cheese.

We'd been an 'item' for four weeks and everyone at the college knew, students and staff alike. Lisa had made sure it didn't remain a secret and I knew it would have been around the building once Joe knew. He'd made a point of wishing us both luck in front of the staff at his leaving do, as he stood swaying on a table in the George and Dragon.

"You've all been schmashing friends, well mohst of you." He raised his glass. "To Gary and Lisha. Hope you'll be very happy together." All the staff looked at us and raised their glasses, chanting 'To Gary and Lisa' and wondering why they hadn't been told previously. Of course, for the rest of that night and the whole of the following week we were the talk of the college and Lisa took great pride in waiting for me in the car park every morning so we could walk in together. I still hadn't stayed at her place during the week though was spending my weekends there, much to mum's relief as it meant Terry could stay over at ours. They'd also become quite serious and I could see mum was getting in deep, talking about them possibly having a future together and maybe even moving in together. Where I'd fit into her plans I wasn't sure, but my twenty-eighth birthday was fast approaching and I knew I needed to stop relying on her so much.

"I think me and Terry might get a place together soon," she'd said one night when we were watching The One Show and they were doing a report on the housing market.

"Where?" I asked, wondering what was wrong with the house she already lived in.

"I'm not sure yet but he's mentioned the bungalows on Hill Crescent, you know, the ones where your Auntie Margaret lived. There are some nice ones on that road and some are pretty big too, with big gardens."

"So are you thinking of selling this place then?"

"I haven't a clue yet, son. Terry only mentioned it the other night. Don't worry though, I won't throw you out." She looked at me and grinned. "And it isn't going to happen overnight. I don't intend rushing into it until I'm absolutely sure it's what I want. To be honest, I didn't think I'd meet anyone else after I threw your dad out. But Terry's opened my eyes, made me see that I'm too young to dwell on the sham of a marriage I had with your dad. And besides, your dad lives with another woman and he's happy enough."

That was true, he *was* happy. The last time I'd seen him was in the White Horse about six months ago where he was having a drink with Gloria, his girlfriend. She seemed nice enough, nothing like mum though. Very blonde and too much makeup, but she invited me to sit down and join them before turning to dad and saying, "You didn't tell me Gary was so gorgeous, darling."

I shook dad's hand and patted him on the shoulder before returning to the bar where Alfie was waiting with a pint for me. Really, I was happy for dad. I hadn't thought there was anything wrong with his and mums marriage until she threw him out for lying about the redundancy, and I felt sorry for him for a while. But I felt I had to remain loyal to mum, she needed me more than dad did, well, maybe at the time.

I knew I'd see dad around occasionally but there had been times recently when I'd wanted to go and see him, have a father-to-son chat about women, Lisa in particular. The news that mum and Terry had been talking about getting a place together had kind of highlighted my concerns a little because, even though I was trying not to admit it to myself, I had thought about asking Lisa if I could move in with her. Her house had two big bedrooms and there was plenty of room for the both of us. I had a feeling she'd be over the moon if I asked, rather than have her ask me and make it look as though she were desperate.

Since Joe had left and I'd got on with my new job as Head of Communications, I'd settled into it really well and was enjoying the challenge of a new post. But I was getting tired of going to Lisa's during the week and having to get dressed again only to drag my arse back home, and most nights to find mum and Terry snuggling up on the settee. It just didn't feel like my home anymore and even Alfie had commented when he came round one night for a piss up with Jez.

"You need your own place, mate," he'd said. "You're too old to be living with your mum."

"I'd love my own place. I just don't like the idea of the bills that go with it."

"But you're paying your mum rent aren't you? You won't be paying much more if you had your own place."

"What about Lisa?" Jez asked. "Don't you want to move in with her?"

"Maybe one day," I replied, noticing Alfie snigger. I suspected he'd never grow up.

"I'm thinking of asking Angela to move in with me." Jez's sudden announcement made Alfie snort beer all over the chair.

"Fuck off," he said, wiping the beer away with his sleeve. "You disappoint me, Jez. Thought you'd be a bachelor forever."

"Not me, mate," Jez replied. "Angela and I are in love. It's time we took our relationship one step further."

"And you're ready to move in together are you?" I asked.

"Yeah, I think so. I know we haven't been seeing each other that long but she stays over at least three nights a week and has a wardrobe full of clothes in the spare room. We can only give it a try can't we?"

I nodded. "Definitely, mate. I say go for it. If I had my own place I'd ask Lisa to move in with me. And I'm pretty sure she would."

"Don't you think she'll ask you to live with her?"

"She might, but this new job is paying well and if she sold her place we could club together and get our own house."

Alfie tutted. "Got it all worked out, haven't you. Never thought I'd see the day." He shook his head and opened another can of Budweiser. "Why don't you have a look around my area? I'm sure there are a couple of pads for sale in the same block."

"I doubt Lisa would want to live your end of town. She likes this end better."

"She likes *your* end, you mean." Alfie laughed at his own joke.

"You're a *bell* end, but yeah, she likes it better my side of town."

And so the seed was planted in my mind; with mum and Terry talking about moving in together it was possible I might be able to convince Lisa to sell her two up-two down and club in with me so that we could buy mum's house. It was worth considering, I thought, as I planned a trip to the off licence to buy a bottle of Cava just in case she said yes.

I went into the classroom to have lunch with her, sitting at a student desk side by side, probably appearing to others like two students cavorting. I arranged to go round to her house that night when I would ask the question. To say I was nervous was an understatement. She answered the door looking every bit lovely in a silk blouse and jeans, her hair up in a pony tail and a smell of roast chicken coming from the kitchen.

"Are you staying tonight," she asked, as I followed her through.

"If you want me to?"

She put her arms around my neck and kissed me. "Of course I want you to, you know that." She pulled away and took some plates from the cupboard. "I want to ask you something after dinner."

"Sounds ominous," I replied, tearing a piece of breast from the chicken and placing it in my mouth.

"It's important. But for now, let's sit down and eat. I've been slaving in this kitchen since I got home and it's been a long day as well." We sat at opposite ends of the small kitchen table. "You know one of my students, Casey Bracknell?" I nodded. "She's pregnant. I'm so disappointed in her. She's got a really bright future ahead of her as well. Doing really well in her studies and now she's made this announcement. She's decided to leave the course at the end of term and I'm gutted."

Casey Bracknell was a tart, in my opinion. She strutted around the college in either tight jeans, shorts or mini-skirts, and the tops she wore often just about covered a nipple. She had long golden hair, wore far too much makeup and had dated just about every boy at college, and I reckon some of the male staff, too. To hear she was pregnant didn't surprise me one bit, but I could tell Lisa was upset. Lisa took her job very seriously and felt it a personal failure on her part if any of her students dropped out or didn't do well. I leant over the table and took hold of her hand.

"Really, sweetheart, I don't think it's surprising news if I'm honest. I would have predicted that a while ago, in fact, I would have predicted it not long after she joined the college twelve months ago. I wouldn't be too worried about her, it's not your fault."

Lisa looked at me. "Well I feel as though it is my fault. I've tried to encourage her to study more and think I might have gone overboard. She's quite clever and when she puts her mind to it she can get through a whole module in a week. This has been a shock to me."

"Sorry, babe, didn't mean to belittle you. Let's not talk about work and enjoy our meal together."

Lisa nodded and looked at her food, picking up her knife and fork. Just like me, nothing deterred her from a meal.

We finished our food and washed up then I put the kettle on and made us both a coffee, carrying them into the lounge where Lisa was sat on the sofa watching Emmerdale. I sidled up to her and shuffled her underneath my arm, kissing the top of her silky head.

"Thanks for that meal, it was lovely, just like you," I said, as she pulled herself up and looked into my eyes. "Didn't you have something to ask me?"

"Yeah, I did. I do, I mean. I was thinking that, well, we've been together now for about, err, five weeks or so and I think we're really, like, close, wouldn't you say?" I nodded. "Well, I was wondering," she stopped.

"What's the matter, babe? Are you okay?"

"Why don't you move in with me?" She blurted it out, just about giving me chance to blink.

I grinned, full of emotion, though a little bit ashamed she was asking me to move in with her and it wasn't the other way around. "I'd love to," I said, watching her eyes light up like two hundred-watt bulbs.

"Oh my god, that's fantastic." She flung her arms around me and hugged me, nearly squeezing the life out of me.

I was admittedly in a state of shock for half an hour or so afterwards, as she chunnered away to herself making plans for where my stuff would go. I would no longer be a true bachelor, looking out for my next notch on the bedpost, wondering if it was going to be her place or mine. The worst part of it was going to be telling Alfie, who'd probably laugh hysterically at me and tell me how sad I was. Jez, I was sure would understand, and then there was mum. She liked Lisa. On the times she'd been to our house, mum had made a special effort to welcome her, regaling her with embarrassing stories about when I was little. It went without saying that Lisa's house wasn't somewhere I'd have chosen to live on my own or if we'd been looking for a place together, but it was an easy option. I just needed to sort out some boxes for my stuff and ask the lads to help me move.

"Of course, you don't need to move in straight away," Lisa said. "You can just move your stuff in gradually if you like, unless your mum would prefer you to move in properly all at once."

"I'm sure mum won't mind either way. I'll get some boxes together this weekend and start moving things over next week, how's that?"

"Sounds perfect." She snuggled into me again. "You're perfect," she said, reaching up to kiss me. "Now let's get up those stairs and celebrate."

I'd left the bottle of Cava in the car, didn't want to look too optimistic when I first arrived and make Lisa think we already had something to celebrate, but I decided to go and fetch it while she went upstairs and got into bed. I took it into the kitchen, popped the cork then poured it into two wine glasses as I couldn't find any champagne flutes. When I got to Lisa's bedroom that would soon be our bedroom, she was lying under the duvet, the top of her breasts poking out in temptation.

"What's the champagne for?" she asked. "Surely you didn't know I was going to ask you to move in?"

I laughed and handed her a glass as she sat up and took it from me. "No, I'm not psychic. Actually, I wanted to ask you something as well and brought it just in case you said yes."

She took a sip then pulled back the duvet to reveal her nakedness. "What?"

I stripped off and joined her in bed, caressing her nipple as she looked at me. "Well, mum and Terry have been talking of getting a place of their own and I had this crazy idea that if they did that, you could put this place up for sale and we could club together to buy mum's house." I dropped a bit of champagne from my glass onto Lisa's nipple then licked it off. "What do you think?"

"Don't you want to live here with me?"

"Of course I do, but I was going to ask you before you asked me. And anyway, mum isn't going anywhere yet, if ever, so it might not have happened at all. But I just thought I'd ask if you would ever want to move in with me." She was staring at me, a twinkle in her eye and a smile dancing on her lips mischievously.

"There are so many reasons why I love you, Gary Stringer. One of them is because you have the biggest cock I've ever seen, but the main one is because you're the most caring and considerate man I've ever known."

"I like the cock reason best," I grinned. She put her hand under the duvet, wrapped her fingers around it, and began moving at a steady rhythm. Her knack for doing that was second to none. Within seconds my cock was standing to attention and in Lisa's mouth, throwing me into ecstasy. It seemed my life was moving on and I was finally turning a new leaf.

Chapter Sixteen

I moved into Lisa's a few weeks later. When I told mum she seemed a bit surprised and asked me to wait a few weeks because we'd only been seeing each other a short time.

"It isn't that long ago you were mad on that Janice girl. I think you should wait before you start moving your stuff in, just give it more time, make sure it's definitely what you want."

"It is what I want," I whinged, like a little boy who was being refused a bag of sweets. "Lisa and I are in love. This is it, mum. Thought you'd be happy for me, settling down at last?"

"I'm more than happy for you, son. But I'm worried about you too. I don't want you to move out of here then six months down the line find you've made a mistake and want to come back, and in the meantime I'll probably have sold the house."

"Does that mean you and Terry are getting a place together then?"

Mum smiled. "It's looking like it, yeah. We had a chat

about it the other night and he's getting Castles to come and do a valuation."

I glared at her. "But you've only been seeing Terry a short time haven't you? Not much longer than I've been with Lisa."

At least she had the grace to blush. "Touché," she laughed. "I know what it looks like, but I'm a lot older than you and this could be my last chance at happiness. Terry's good for me, he has a great job, money in the bank and a very nice house, and he said I could move in with him anytime."

"So is that what you're doing?"

"I might do, yes. Though I'd prefer to see you settled first."

I walked towards mum and hugged her. No matter what either of us did, I always came first in her life and for that, I loved her more than I could say.

"I want you to be happy, mum," I said, drawing away and holding her hands. I looked down at a few liver spots that seemed to have materialised on her skin. "Looks like we've both got a new life to look forward to."

"You're right, we have, but we'll always be here for each other, eh?"

"You bet we will." I hugged her again then left the room, hoping she hadn't seen the tears prickling my eyes. I might have been in my late twenties and looking forward to moving in with my girlfriend, but my mum would always be number one in my life.

⬤ ～⟨⟩～ ⬤

Lisa was beside herself with excitement during the run up week before I moved in. Jez helped me move my stuff by borrowing a van from work and Alfie, much to my disappointment, stayed away. I was a bit pissed off with him really as he'd shown no enthusiasm for me when I'd told him and Jez about moving in with Lisa. Jez shook my hand and patted me on the back.

"I'm fucking thrilled for you, mate. Hope you'll be really happy. Angela's moving in with me next week, just got a few things to finalise then it's all systems go."

"That's great news, Jez." I looked at Alfie who was examining his finger nails. "You next, eh?" I said, trying to at least get him to acknowledge mine and Jez's good news.

"Never in a million years will I live with a bird. Fuck 'em and leave 'em, that's me, till the death." And with that he stood up and went to fetch some more cans from the fridge. Jez and I knew it was better to leave him to it, though I suspected he was jealous of our happy news.

Lisa had emptied one of her wardrobes ready for all my stuff though I had quite a lot of my clothes already at her house. I wanted to bring my desk and laptop plus all my CDs, DVDs and books that I'd collected over the years. Her house wasn't over big for all our stuff together but we crammed everything in somehow. We decided not to bother unpacking my boxes just in case mum decided to sell her house as we'd both agreed that to sell Lisa's place and club together to buy mum's made sense.

Everyone at work was thrilled for us and I have to say I felt better that it was all out in the open. Students were congratulating us on moving in together and even Lisa's troubled student Casey Bracknell, who was now four months pregnant, came up to me and said I was a very lucky man. I had to agree; I was very lucky indeed.

Our first night living together had us making love till the early hours as we sipped on champagne in between oral sex. It was all pretty magical and my new life as a man in a relationship was proving to be just what I needed. Lisa fell asleep in my arms that night and I kissed the top of her head, whispering 'I love you' as she slept soundly against my chest.

A couple of weeks after I'd moved in with Lisa I decided to nip into Jack's cafe and buy myself and Lisa a sandwich for lunch. Janice hadn't entered my thoughts for weeks and I knew I was well and truly over her. She meant nothing to me anymore, not since Lisa and I had made plans for our future. I hadn't even had an incline to go to the cafe and had carried on making a packed lunch, though once I'd moved in with Lisa, she made it for me. However, this particular Wednesday we'd overslept after a heavy night of passion and I found myself walking through the door of Jack's.

I noticed Billy Brown first, stood behind the counter serving a customer. Then I saw Janice, putting a cup of something onto a table in front of a young good looking guy. I noticed how she flirted with him and how he followed her wiggling arse all the way back to the counter where Billy was scowling. As I neared her she looked up and saw me.

"Hi, Gary," she chirped. "I haven't seen you in here for ages. How are you?"

"I'm good, thanks. How are you?"

"Almost ready to emigrate, thank heavens. It's been a long couple of months but I'm getting there."

"When do you go?" I noticed how soft her skin was and how a few strands of hair fell loosely by the side of her face, framing her features like a porcelain doll.

"Next week. I've got my ticket booked. It's my last day here tomorrow."

"That's come round quickly. It'll seem strange in here without your smiling face."

"What can I get you," she asked, her gorgeous white teeth gleaming at me.

"One cheese and pickle on white and a prawn

cocktail on brown please."

"Treating someone to lunch are you?" She turned around to grab some rolls from the shelf.

"Yeah, my girlfriend, Lisa."

She turned back to face me and put the rolls down. I wasn't sure if it was disappointment on her face or shock, but it made me feel a little uncomfortable.

"I didn't know you had a girlfriend. How long have you been together?" She started buttering the rolls.

"A couple of months now. We live together."

Janice put the butter knife down and went to the trays where sandwich fillings were displayed behind a glass counter. She picked up a spoon and filled the brown roll with prawn cocktail, wrapped it in a bag, placed it on the counter then took the white roll and filled that one with cheese and pickle. I was biting my lip wondering if I should say something as the atmosphere had become extremely tense.

"That's nice, I'm glad you're settling down." She put my cheese and pickle roll on the counter then tallied up the amount on the till. "Four pounds, thirty, please." She held out her hand and waited for my five pound note.

"I hope things work out for you in Australia, Janice," I said, as she handed me the change.

"I had hoped I'd see you again before I went but I realise that's out of the question now. Thanks, Gary, see you around then."

I stood for a moment and glared at her. She really was a very attractive woman and the fact she seemed disappointed at me not arranging another date with her confused me somewhat.

"After I saw you in Banana's with that guy I assumed you'd found someone else." I tried to make light of it, etching a chuckle into my voice.

She looked puzzled for a second. "That guy is my cousin. He works in Banana's. He's a bouncer. I go in there sometimes when I'm bored and he gets me free drinks."

Shit. Was I an arsewipe or what? "Oh right, it's just that you looked quite cosy together so I thought, you know, you'd moved on." I noticed Billy Brown standing close by, no doubt ear-wigging.

"It's okay, I know there would never have been a future for us with me moving away. I couldn't expect you to hang around waiting to see if I changed my mind. I'm happy that you've found someone else. You deserve to be happy."

I smiled awkwardly. "I'm sorry, Janice," I said, not really knowing what I had to be sorry about. It was, after all, she who'd told me that she didn't want to get too involved. "Maybe if you hadn't been emigrating we could have had something?"

"I'm sure we could have." She turned her head and looked towards another customer who was now standing tapping his fingers on the top of the counter with impatience.

"I'll see you, Janice," I said, then turned and made my way to the door. As I opened it I looked back towards the counter only to see her staring straight at me, a glistening in her eyes as though she was close to tears.

That night after seeing Janice I got in from work and hugged Lisa, tempted to stay attached to her body for the rest of my days. Eventually she pulled away, obviously realising that something was on my mind. I'd psyched myself up all afternoon, trying hard not to let her see that I was affected because I knew I'd only have to lie to her. I was Gary, new man with a new life, and I didn't want to start telling lies in our first months of living together only to have her never trust me again. Dad had lied to mum about the redundancy, and God knows whatever else, and I sure had no intention of living a life where I couldn't talk to Lisa about things that were on my mind.

To be fair to mum, and as I looked back over their marriage, I'd started to understand that she had been living a bit of a dog's life with dad. He'd often taken her out and they'd spent weekends away occasionally, but it was always what *he* wanted. I remember one year when they went to Cornwall for a fortnight and mum had really wanted to go to Italy. Dad said he hated Italy even though he'd never been and told mum it was either Cornwall or nowhere. She knew not to argue with him, there would have been little point, so off they went after mum had done all the packing whilst dad stayed out of the way, propping up the bar in the George and Dragon.

When they got back from the holiday mum was knackered. Dad had booked them into a cottage near a beach resort and because he wasn't over keen on the food that was served in the restaurants nearby, mum had ended up cooking for them most nights. She'd also had to make several trips to the dry cleaners because dad drank too much and kept barfing everywhere. They ended up paying out a few hundred pounds to get the cottage cleaned after the stench of dad's vomit had overwhelmed the place. And that few hundred pounds came out of mum's pay packet.

I'd always looked up to him as a young child, thought he was my hero. He'd take me to football matches sometimes and watch from the sidelines as I struggled to kick a ball around the playing field. I couldn't stand football when I was a kid but dad insisted I played for the local boy's team so he could brag about me in the pub. Thing is, there was nothing to brag about because I was always on the bench.

Lisa looked into my eyes as she pulled away from me, her hands cupped around my face. "What's wrong, babe?" She stroked my face with her finger.

"Oh, nothing." Here we go, I thought. "Just had a long day. I'll be fine after a beer."

Lisa reached into the fridge and passed me a can of Stella. "Here you are, honey, I'll sort dinner out, you go and relax. Why don't you get in the bath for a bit?"

"Will you join me?"

"Only if you're not interested in dinner?"

"Hmmm, difficult one," I said, pulling her towards me again and planting my lips heavily on hers. "I'll go and watch telly for a bit, that'll relax me."

"Dinner will be in half an hour, sweetpea."

Lisa called me some great names, much nicer than I'd ever been called before. I often wondered how Alfie would feel if a bird addressed him as 'sweetpea' or 'honey'. I reckon he'd run a mile. And perhaps six months ago I would have done, too. But not now. I was finding this new me quite pleasant and I was enjoying living with Lisa more than I thought I would ever enjoy living with a girl.

We had a quiet night in after dinner, just a quick session when we went to bed then the usual cuddles before sleep. I dreamt about Janice that night; she came to our house, knocked on the door and asked to speak to me when Lisa answered. I was hovering in the front room, looking for somewhere to hide. When Lisa let her in I was sat on the television, Eggheads blaring up my arse as I watched Janice's face slowly turn into Alfie's. I had some really weird dreams.

Chapter Seventeen

*T*he weekend came and went and I was ashamed to admit that Janice had been on my mind far too much. I didn't go to the cafe on her last day which was Thursday because I really didn't want to have unwanted feelings rushing to the surface, knowing I had a beautiful woman at home who wanted me far more than Janice ever would. But the fact she was on my mind was starting to eat away at me and I knew it was only a matter of time before Lisa would comment on my distant mood. It was Monday night when we got home from work and she offered to get us a Chinese.

"I'm not hungry," I answered, wondering which day Janice would be emigrating. She'd told me it would be this week but hadn't told me the actual day.

"You seem very distant recently, what's up?" She joined me on the sofa and sidled up to me. I lifted my arm up and dropped it around her shoulder.

"Nothing's up, babe. I'm fine." I kissed the top of her head. "Honest."

"You would tell me if you weren't happy, wouldn't

you?"

"I am happy, sweetheart. I've never been happier. You only need to ask the lads that!"

"I know. But I can't help feeling you've got something on your mind that you're not prepared to tell me. We're a partnership now. You and me all the way." She looked at me, her beautiful dark brown eyes staring into mine. I swept her into my arms and hugged her tightly, reminding myself how lucky I was, how incredibly fortunate I'd been to find someone as amazing as Lisa. I knew Janice shouldn't be entering my head anymore and perhaps the feelings I was showing Lisa were of guilt.

Suddenly, something came over me, as though I had a sudden urge to make everything alright, bring all my worries and past experiences to a head and take the final step to being the new Gary Stringer. I got off the sofa and knelt down on the floor in front of Lisa, taking hold of both her hands. I glared straight into her eyes as a smile danced on her lips. I reckon she assumed I was after sex but my ideas went far beyond a quickie in the front room.

"Lisa," I began, clearing my throat, a little anxiety causing the beginnings of heartburn. "Lisa, you know I love you. I feel like the luckiest guy on earth living here with you." On any other occasion, it would have sounded vomit-inducing. "What we have has turned my life around and made me see that I like being who I am and I love being a part of your life." She smiled and nodded at me, probably wondering what was wrong with me. I continued, "Anyway, what I'm trying to say, trying to ask, is, Lisa Hill, will you marry me?" I even shocked myself. I could see she was taken aback when she leant back against the sofa but then the tears came, hers, and she suddenly flung her arms around me and hugged the life out of me. "Is that a yes?" I asked, hoping I hadn't made a complete tit of myself.

"Of course it's a yes. Oh my god, we're getting married. Me and you. Oh my god." She was excited, I could tell. "Oh wow, I've got so much to do. I'll need to make lists, choose some dates, buy a wedding dress, choose rings." She squeezed me again. "You've made me the happiest person alive. I love you so much." Then she ripped off her blouse, threw off her jeans and somehow straddled me on the floor whilst I still knelt in front of her. It all happened so fast.

"If this is the reaction I get when I ask you to marry me, I'm going to ask you every day!" I said, climbing out of my jeans and pulling my t-shirt over my head.

"You can ask me as much as you want, you lovely, lovely man."

Suffice to say Lisa and I made love that night like we'd never done before. We were now a couple on a mission, a mission to get married and spend the rest of our lives together, maybe even have kids one day, and that night was the happiest night of my life to date.

We told mum the following day after work and she was thrilled to bits. She hugged Lisa and welcomed her into the family and I could tell that Lisa was truly happy when she said to mum, "You're going to be my mother-in-law, it'll be like having a second mum."

"You can call me mum if you like," mum said, then looked at me and nodded.

I shrugged and looked at Lisa. "Ooh, I don't know," she said. "Maybe I'll just call you Christine for now and then once we're married I can call you mum."

"Sounds good to me. Have you told your parents yet?"

"Not yet, no. We'll go and see them this weekend."

Shit, I thought, I'm going to meet my in-laws and I've

never met them before. The times Lisa had been to visit them she'd always gone on her own and they hadn't been to see us yet. I kind of assumed they weren't very impressed with their only daughter living in-sin with someone but Lisa kept telling me they just wanted her to be happy. I'd have to make a good first impression, I knew that, but the thought of shaking her dad's hand made me think of Janice again and that time I went to pick her up from home to take her to Luciano's, when her dad greeted me at the front door.

And thinking of Janice, I suddenly realised it was Wednesday tomorrow and she might well have already left for Australia. A part of me wanted to know if she had gone but I knew I needed to listen to the sensible side of my brain for a change and stop thinking about her now that my life had moved on to another level.

Mum made us a delicious beef curry and whilst she and Lisa discussed wedding venues and styles of dresses over the table, I moved into the front room, leaving the women to their plans. I had wondered if I'd get a say in any of it at some point but I could see how excited Lisa was about the whole thing. The fact I wouldn't have known where to start planning a wedding made me realise it was best if I just left them to it. By the end of the night they'd made a guest list of all our families, friends and work colleagues, had sorted out where the disco would be held, who would do the catering and where we'd have the wedding breakfast. It was gone eleven o'clock when we said goodbye to mum and though Lisa was still buzzing with excitement, I was most definitely ready for bed.

When we got in I went straight upstairs and stripped off then climbed into bed and snuggled up, glad to be able to close my eyes. Just as I was drifting off to sleep my mobile buzzed on the bedside table next to me. It was a text message. More alarmingly, it was a text message from Janice.

"Who's that texting you at this time?" Lisa asked, turning around to see me getting out of bed with the phone in my hand.

"It's one of those PPI messages. I'll switch it off."

I took the phone into the bathroom and sat on the toilet seat.

"Hi Gary, sorry to text you so late, I know you don't want to hear from me now that you're with someone, but I just wanted to let you know that I'm at the airport and my plane's due to leave in an hour. I'm glad we got to know each other a little but I'm sorry we didn't get closer. I really did like you and I think you liked me too. Anyway, hope things work out for you with your new girlfriend. I'm happy to stay in touch if you like but will understand if you don't text back. Love Janice x

To say I was in shock was an understatement. I honestly didn't think I'd get a text from Janice, especially as I hadn't been back to the cafe to see her. But despite me being shocked at her getting in touch, I was actually relieved that she had. I hovered over the keys, thinking frantically of a suitable reply before Lisa would come knocking on the bathroom door wondering if mum's curry had given me the shits because I'd been in there so long.

"Hi Janice, really great to hear from you. Sorry I didn't manage to see you before you left. I'm really glad you've finally made it to the airport, a new life in Oz, how exciting for you. It would be nice to keep in touch though I'm sure you'll want to get settled. Have a good flight and a great life over there. Take care, Gary x"

That sounded okay, I thought, as I hit 'send', watching the little airplane symbol appear on the screen as the text was bouncing into Janice's phone. I knew it wouldn't be easy to keep in touch with her, even though it would have been nice, but I had to let her go, get on with my new life and not dwell on what could have been. Lisa was my future, Janice was my past. And really, when I thought about it properly, Janice hadn't even been in my past for that long. She'd just been a girl I'd fancied, someone who was good in bed, nice arse, nice tits, nice personality. Another notch on the bedpost, that incidentally, was still at mum's.

I had to forget about her, maybe even think about deleting her number from my phone. Maybe, I thought, I should block her number to prevent her contacting me again, that way we would both be forced to make this fresh start and not have any lingering doubts hanging over us. It was a past that hadn't really been much to talk about and it would never have been anything like what Lisa and I had now.

I made my way back to the bedroom where Lisa lay curled up under the duvet, softly breathing as she slept like a baby. I snuggled into her and she stirred a little so I held back, afraid to wake her. It was almost midnight and we both had to be up at seven for work.

Chapter Eighteen

*T*hat weekend we went to Lisa's parents' house in the Cotswolds. The driveway alone took my breath away as it swept towards a quaint thatched-roof cottage hidden amongst the trees. A large garden at the front of the house growing wild flowers, had a pond situated in the centre with a cherub fountain and lily pads in the water. Lisa's mum was standing at the front door when we arrived and she waved madly as we drew up behind a very nice Jaguar.

"Darling," sang my future mother-in-law, her arms outstretched as Lisa ran into them. "It's so lovely to have you both here. Where's this handsome young man of yours?" She looked towards me as I was locking the car.

I strode casually in her direction, noticing a string of pearls around her neck and very glossy red lipstick. She was actually a good looking woman and it seemed she was very pleased to see me. I held out my hand and she took it in both of hers.

"Hello, Gary, we've heard such a lot about you. I can't believe we've finally got to meet you. Come in,

Philip's in the back garden, I don't think he knows you're here. Knowing him, he'll be locked in his shed having a crafty cigarette, even though the doctor has told him time and time again to give up. Do you smoke?"

"Just occasionally," I answered, hoping Philip wasn't going to invite me into his shed for a crafty fag and a man to man chat.

"Oh well, you and Philip will get on like a house on fire." She ushered us through the impressive hallway with a low beamed ceiling and oozing character, into a small room that seemed cluttered with a bureau, leather bound arm chair and a book shelf, with patio doors at one end. She opened the doors and we all stepped into an oasis of greenery, rockery and vibrant flowers. It looked more like a garden centre than someone's back garden, but it was certainly very beautiful and a credit to Lisa's mum and dad.

"Philip, they're here." The door to the small shed that stood at the bottom of the garden swung open and a man in his fifties appeared, a cigarette in one hand and a mug in the other. I already liked the look of him and I hadn't even met him.

He rushed over to us, stubbing the cigarette out and threw the end into the bushes as he walked past them.

"Philip, you can jolly well go and pick that up. You have an ashtray in your shed." He ignored the command and continued to walk towards us all, hugging Lisa as he reached us.

"Hi, dad." She turned around to face me. "This is Gary."

Philip held out his hand and I took it in mine He had a very firm handshake and a great beaming smile on his face. "Very good to meet you. I'm sorry we haven't managed to get up to you but this bloody bad back I have is making it hard for me to get up in the mornings. Anyway, great that you're here, lad, maybe we can get to know each other a bit better once these ladies have gone inside to put the kettle on, eh?" He nudged me and winked. I liked Philip, he was my kind of guy.

"Sounds good to me, Mr. Hill," I replied.

"Mr. Hill? Who the bloody hell's Mr. Hill?" he asked, a bellowing laugh rising from his belly. He slapped me on the back. "Call me Philip, for goodness sake." He looked at his wife. "You can call her what you want but she usually answers to Margie. Ha-ha."

I laughed too and looked at Margie who was shaking her head and trying not to scowl.

"Gary, will you help me with the case?" Lisa asked as she took hold of my hand and pulled me back inside. I had no choice but to follow obligingly; this making a good impression on her parents meant I must be seen to be at their daughter's beck and call every minute of the day.

"Right, while you're doing that I'll make us a nice pot of tea and butter some fresh scones. You two go and make yourselves comfortable." She turned to Philip. "You come with me *after* you've picked up that disgusting cigarette stub." She then turned on her heels and followed us inside.

Lisa led me upstairs to a front bedroom with its own bathroom. It was a good size double room with built-in wardrobes and a slant in the roof. I did think about bashing my head in the middle of the night and made a mental note of where the slant finished and where my head would hit should I get up quickly without thinking where I was. The best thing to do would be not to have too much to drink, that way I wouldn't need to get up all night for the loo and wouldn't be disorientated when I did.

I pushed Lisa onto the bed and lay on top of her, cradling her in my arms. "This is a gorgeous house," I said, "you didn't tell me your mum and dad lived in such a lovely area. Don't fancy my chances with that low ceiling though."

She laughed and kissed me on my cheek before pushing me away and getting off the bed. "I think you should have a chat with my dad before we make our wedding announcement."

"What do you mean?"

"Well, you know, ask his permission. I'm his only daughter, you know they don't see my brother Alan anymore, and I think he'll really respect you for asking rather than just assuming we've got their blessing."

I could feel my stomach being tied in knots. "What if he says no?"

"He won't say no, you numpty. He knows how much I love you and how much you love me. You just need to make him realise that you're in this for better or worse, so to speak; that you intend to look after me like he's done all these years with my mum, and that you'll be an amazing son-in-law. You know, that type of thing."

"I've never done anything like this before. I'm nervous."

Lisa laughed again. I was starting to get a complex. "Don't be silly, of course you haven't done this before and you're bound to be nervous. That'll impress dad even more if he knows you're nervous."

"You make your dad sound like Hitler."

She put her arms around my neck. "Listen, I know mum and dad like you, I can tell, and they've only just met you. I haven't brought many boys home before and they've been banging on at me for ages now to settle down, so once dad realises how serious we are about each other, he'll be thrilled for us. Honestly, darling, I promise."

"If he says he won't give permission I'll throttle you."

"If he says no I'll throttle *you*, because that'll only mean one thing, that he doesn't trust you, and if he doesn't trust you I'll need to know why. My dad has a sixth sense, he can judge people really well by first impressions and I reckon you've made a great first impression on him. Now stop worrying and go and talk to him. And when you have, come back and tell me how it went then we'll tell mum."

I kissed her, unable to resist her cherry lips, then left her in the bedroom unpacking our case. We were only staying a couple of nights but she'd brought enough to last us at least a week.

Margie was in the kitchen buttering hot scones that smelt delicious and Philip was in an adjoining room that I later found out was known as the 'morning room'. I was starting to suspect that Lisa's mum and dad weren't short of a bob or two and our wedding might just be covered by their bank account. It wouldn't have bothered me to have paid for it all ourselves of course, but having their contribution would certainly help. The wedding my mum and Lisa had planned the other night was quickly turning into a celebrity wedding of the century and I knew at some point I'd have to get more involved if only to reduce the guest list and remind Lisa that we weren't millionaires.

I went into the morning room to join Philip, my palms sweaty and my knees starting to wobble. I thought I'd be at least in my thirties before I had to ask a girl's father permission to marry her but there I was, almost twenty eight and asking a question that I hoped I'd only ever need to ask once in my life.

"Come and sit down, Gary," Philip said, patting the chair next to him. I did as I was told. "We can have a wander around the garden this afternoon, have a good chat and get to know each other properly. I have to say, my little girl seems very happy with you, lad. You're obviously good for her."

I smiled, getting ready for my life changing question to pop out. I cleared my throat and scratched my nose, wanting to scratch my balls as well but thinking better of it. Here goes, I thought, it's now or never...

"Philip, do you want strawberry jam or raspberry on

your scone?" Margie called from the kitchen just as the words were going to leave my mouth.

"Oh, that damn woman," Philip laughed. "Love her to bits but you'd think after thirty-five years of marriage she'd know I prefer strawberry jam on my buttered scones."

I nodded nervously and tried to laugh, though it came out as a choirboy chuckle.

"Strawberry, darling." He looked at me and shook his head. "Women, eh, can't live with them, can't live without them."

"Yeah, right, I know what you mean." I cleared my throat again. "Thing is, Philip, I need to ask you something important and I'm a bit nervous to be honest."

"Spit it out, lad, don't be an idiot."

"Well, err, you see, Lisa and I, we love each other very much and feel very content together. The thing is, Philip, that I want to spend the rest of my life with your daughter and I'd like your permission to marry her." I scrambled out the words, stumbling over half of them and for a moment I wondered if he would have understood me. I stared at him, hoping his reaction would change from being in shock to showing at least some happiness for us.

I must have caught him on a good day. He stood up and reached out his hand. I stood up opposite him and put my hand in his, letting him shake it vigorously as he grinned from ear to ear.

"Well, well, lad, I never thought I'd see the day, my little girl bringing home a fully grown man with manners. I'd be honoured to have you as my son-in-law, and you most definitely have my permission to marry my daughter." He slapped me on the back, forcing me a few inches forward. "Bugger me, this causes for a celebration." He skipped to the door. "I'll open a bottle of champagne."

I couldn't believe it, I'd done it. I'd taken one step further to becoming a new man, a married man of all things, one with responsibilities and in-laws, and a wife. Oh my god, I would have a wife. How bizarre did that sound? What the hell would Alfie and Jez make of that news? I could imagine Jez being happy for me but Alfie's attitude had been a bit off recently and I wasn't looking forward to telling him I would soon be a married man.

Just as Philip came out of the cellar with a bottle of champagne, Lisa appeared at the kitchen door, her mum spreading jam on the scones. I peered through the door of the morning room and smiled at her, nodding. She jumped up and squealed then came to me, flinging her arms around my neck and kissing me wildly.

"Shall I tell mum, or do you want to?" she asked.

"I think it'd be best coming from you," I said, watching as Margie stopped spreading the jam and looked towards us both.

"Tell me what?" she asked, waving a knife about.

Philip popped the champagne cork and reached for four flutes out of a glass fronted cupboard. "We've got something to celebrate my darling," he said, pouring the champagne. "We're going to have a new member to our family."

Margie thankfully put the knife down and put her hands to her mouth. "You mean... you're not are you?" She looked at Lisa's stomach.

"God no. Oh, mum, what are you like."

"What?" I asked.

"Mum thinks I'm having a baby," Lisa answered, laughing nervously, slipping her arm through mine. "We're getting married, mum. Gary's asked for dad's permission and he's given it. Isn't that wonderful news?"

Margie took her eyes from Lisa's stomach and

stared at me. "You haven't been together that long, when are you planning to get married?"

"We've been together long enough to know we're in love, mum, and that we want to spend the rest of our lives together. Please be happy for us." Lisa gripped my arm and I felt sorry for her. This wasn't the reaction she'd hoped for from her mum.

"Well, I am happy for you, of course I am, but I wish you'd thought this through more, maybe waited until you'd been together for a year or so."

"You and dad got married after a short time didn't you?"

"Things were different back then, Lisa Jayne. It was a different era. Nowadays it's acceptable to live together for a while, test the water to see if making a commitment is really what you want to do."

I walked over to Lisa's mum. "I love your daughter, Margie," I said, "I want to marry her and she wants to marry me. It won't make a difference if it's in twelve months or not."

"And we're not getting married straight away, mum. We've got a lot of planning to do first and people book weddings well in advance these days. We'll probably set a date for next year in the summer."

"Well, I suppose that'll be something at least." Margie wiped her hands on a tea towel. "Oh, come here, of course I'm happy for you." She outstretched her arms and beckoned us towards her. "For both of you. You do look good together and I'm just a silly old bugger." She put her arms around us both, hugging us to her then she turned towards my ear. "You hurt my daughter and I'll come after you and chop your balls off."

I stood back and gave a false chuckle, not sure whether she meant it. Though I had no intention of hurting Lisa, the threat of having my balls chopped off was a good deterrent, I'll give her that.

Philip raised his glass. "To Lisa and Gary." It was quite sweet really, the toast I mean, not the champagne, that was vile. I would have preferred a can of beer but didn't want to offend Philip so I knocked it back in a couple of gulps and accepted another glass.

"You'll have me drunk," I laughed.

"I think you're allowed to have a tipple when you're about to become a married man." He turned to Lisa. "So, any dates in mind yet, darling?"

"We haven't got an engagement ring yet, dad." Lisa looked at me with pleading eyes.

"I was going to take you after work next week, only if you want to though, I mean, no pressure."

"Of course I want to," Lisa said, thumping my chest as her parents laughed at my sarcasm.

"I was thinking of taking you to Harley's."

"Bought an engagement ring from there before, lad?" Philip asked with a snigger.

I jumped back in despair. "Oh, err, no, Philip. I can assure you, Lisa is the first and last girl to be my fiancée."

"Glad to hear it, son." He raised his glass again. "Welcome to the Hill family."

"Thanks, Philip," I choked, relieved that he didn't think I was a serial proposer.

"Harley's sounds fabulous," Lisa purred, kissing my cheek softly. "We could go after work on Monday. I was thinking about a platinum and diamond ring. I do love platinum." She lifted Margie's hand towards me. "Show Gary your ring, mum." Margie flashed a sparkler that shone on her wedding finger. I doubted I'd be able to afford anything like it and I hoped Lisa would realise. "Something like that," she said, with come-to-bed eyes.

"Hmm, well, we can have a look at what they have and if you don't see anything we'll try somewhere else." I bent down to whisper into Lisa's ear. "I won't be able to afford something like your mum's, you do know that don't you?"

"Of course I do, silly. We'll just get what we can afford. It's the twenty-first century, Gary, we can club together on the ring. I don't expect you to fork out for it in full."

Phew, that put my mind at rest, though it still meant Lisa was probably expecting the most expensive ring in the shop.

Chapter Nineteen

I thoroughly enjoyed the rest of the weekend at
Phillip and Margie's. I have to say they made me
very welcome and fussed around Lisa and I like we
were two precious stones. Talking of stones, I managed
to buy, all with my own money, a platinum and diamond
ring for Lisa from Harley's in the sale and it was just
what she wanted, and better still, it didn't break the
bank, not too much anyway. She made a point of
showing it to everyone at work throughout the week and
all the female students were in awe, telling her how
lucky she was to have such a beautiful ring and telling
me how lucky I was to have such a beautiful fiancée.

I hadn't seen much of Alfie for a while though we
seemed to have created a foursome with Jez and Angela
as we all got on really well together and spent most
Friday nights with a takeaway and a few bottles of wine.
They announced they were getting married also but
were waiting a couple of years until they'd saved up
enough to have a proper lavish wedding. I didn't ask any
questions but I got the impression Angela's parents

didn't have much money and as Jez's parents lived in Spain, I guess it must have been difficult for them to plan something soon. As it happened though, Lisa and my mum were hurrying our wedding plans along and Lisa had already bought her dress, stored at mum's, yet we hadn't even set a date.

I did think it was all going a bit quick and against my better judgement decided to tackle Lisa on it one night when we'd just made love on the sofa whilst watching a DVD.

"What do you mean, it's all going a bit quick?" She was none too pleased with my announcement.

I tried to backtrack a little. "Well, like you and mum are making all these plans and I don't feel as though I'm a part of it. And what about your mum and dad? Aren't they paying for everything? Shouldn't they be included in some of the plans as well?"

Lisa sat up and folded her arms. That was a sure sign that I'd pissed her off. "I told you not to worry about things, I'll get it all sorted. All you need to do is look gorgeous and turn up. Do you think you can manage that?"

"I can look gorgeous," I grinned. But unfortunately, Lisa didn't see the funny side of my comment.

"You can be a right knob sometimes, Gary. This wedding is the biggest and most special day of our lives and it's all a big joke to you. Maybe you should just move in with Alfie and play at bachelors together." She stood up, grabbed her empty glass then stormed into the kitchen.

I dithered on the sofa, dressed only in boxer shorts. I hated upsetting her but she was taking the whole thing a bit over the top. I didn't dare ask how much things were costing, mainly because I didn't want her parents to think I was eager to pay any bills.

"I'm sorry, babe, I didn't mean to upset you." I followed her into the kitchen as she slammed cupboard doors. She had a bra and knickers on and looked spectacular, even with the sulky face. "Come here," I pleaded, opening my arms out to her.

"Oh, bugger off. I'm going to bed." And with that she stormed out of the kitchen and stamped upstairs like a five year old, leaving me standing almost naked probably looking like a prize prick.

It took a few days for Lisa to come round after our little tete-a-tete. She turned her back on me in bed and wouldn't even make my sandwiches for lunch so I knew I was in the dog house. It was only when I went to Jack's cafe in the middle of that week that a part of me wished Janice had been there, someone I could have perhaps talked to in a grown up fashion. My birthday was days away and I suspected Lisa hadn't even bought me a card. She certainly hadn't mentioned going out anywhere which I was a bit disappointed about, though mum rang the night before enquiring what we were doing.

"Terry wondered if you'd both like to go to Luciano's, his birthday present to you."

"Oh, right, that's very generous." It *was* generous. A nosh up there for four people would set him back a fair bit. "I think that's very nice of him. I'll ask Lisa later and see what she says."

"Well, it's *your* birthday, surely Lisa will just go along with anything you want for your birthday?" Mum spoke to me as though she suspected I was under the thumb. She wasn't the only one. Alfie had since made it quite clear that I'd become a boring bastard and he wanted the old Gary back.

"I'm sure she'll agree," I assured mum, hoping that Lisa would be speaking to me again that night so I could ask her.

As she wasn't however, I couldn't ask her and so decided to ring mum the next day and tell her we'd meet them there at 8pm. I knew I was taking a chance but it was time Lisa stopped being so childish. I intended putting my foot down thus putting a stop to this silly misunderstanding. She either needed to get a sense of humour or chill out. Either way, I wasn't going to put up with her moods anymore.

Billy Brown was serving behind the counter with a young, dark haired girl, very pretty with blue rimmed glasses on. I recognised her from college; a student who left a few years ago.

"What can I get you," she asked sweetly.

"Cheese and pickle on a white roll and a piece of millionaire shortbread, please."

"You heard from Janice?" Billy was staring at me. I blinked and stood back when he spoke, wondering where he'd got his sudden voice from.

"No, have you?" I asked, taking the roll from the pretty girl's hands.

"Yeah, she texts me all the time."

What a plank. "Does she? That's nice," I said, a false smile hovering on my lips. "How's she doing?"

"She's happier than she was here. Got herself settled, away from the rubbish she had to put up with over here." I refrained from punching him, I was too hungry.

I handed the girl my money and walked off. I knew that afternoon I wouldn't be able to resist texting Janice. There was no way I could get through my day without banging out a few words, just to see how she was. I'd almost deleted her contact from my phone several times, mainly for fear of Lisa seeing the name, but something always held me back. I guess a part of me just wanted to speak to her again.

"Hi Janice, just thought I'd see how you're doing. Hope you've settled in ok, let me know how you are. Gary x"

I contemplated the kiss at the end but without it the text just seemed a bit cold. Then I hit 'send'. Like an obsessive nutter, I must have checked my phone every five minutes for the rest of that day and even left it on the coffee table at home whilst I was watching football. Lisa had gone upstairs to mark some papers. She still wouldn't speak to me and I was getting a bit pissed off with her attitude, thinking if she saw a text from Janice it might spur her on to stop acting like a child. Of course, nothing's ever simple is it?

The football finished and I, knackered and grumpy because my team had lost, went to bed, poking my head around the spare bedroom door to say goodnight to Lisa. She didn't lift her head from the desk so I carried on to our bedroom and snuggled myself under the duvet.

The next morning I was awoken by Lisa prodding me in my arm. Opening my eyes I looked at her and then over at the alarm clock wondering why it hadn't gone off.

"What time is it?" I asked.

"Half-past seven. Are you getting up or what?" At least she was speaking to me again.

"Why don't you come back to bed for five minutes?" She was wearing a tightly fitted polo neck jumper with no sleeves and it was turning me on no end. The duvet must have resembled a tent.

"I'm going to make some toast. Do you want any?"

"Oh." Damn. "Yeah, okay, that'll be nice. Two slices please, sweetheart." I got out of bed and went into the bathroom, splashing cold water on my face before I got under the shower.

Lisa was sat at the kitchen table when I got downstairs, eating toast and reading the newspaper. My stomach sank when I saw my mobile phone on the worktop, remembering I'd left it on the coffee table last night, still switched on.

"You might want to look at that," she said, not lifting her head from the paper.

I picked up a piece of toast and bit into it then picked

up the phone with my other hand and hit the menu key. It was a text message. From Janice.

"Hi Gary, lovely to hear from you again. How are you? I'm really well thanks, have settled great here and made lots of new friends. Haven't got a new boyfriend yet but I'm working on it, lol. I miss you loads and keep thinking about you and what we could have had. Please keep in touch. Love J x"

By the time I'd finished reading Janice's text, Lisa had turned in her chair and was watching me, arms well and truly folded.

"Who the fuck's Janice?" she asked. I rarely heard Lisa say the F word so I knew I was in deep shit.

"She's a friend of mine. She moved to Australia months ago and sometimes we text each other."

"A friend? A friend who keeps thinking about you and what you could have had, who ends her texts with 'Love J'?" Lisa stood up and continued glaring at me. I thought she might hit me at one point so I backed away slightly, holding the toast like a shield with the phone in my other hand

"Lisa, you're blowing this out of proportion. Janice really is a mate. We went out on a date once but it didn't work out and we decided to just stay friends. Honestly, honey, that's all it is." I nervously inched a bit closer to her.

"Have you told her about me? Does she know you're supposed to be getting married?"

"What do you mean, 'supposed to be'? For God sake Lisa, you're making a mountain out of a molehill."

"I mean 'supposed to be' because I'm not really sure it's what you want, is it? You don't seem bothered one bit about this wedding."

I looked at the diamond shining on her finger. "And what do you call that?" I asked. "Isn't that proof that I'm taking this wedding seriously? I asked *you* to marry *me*, don't forget." She couldn't argue with that.

Unfortunately, I realised there and then, that Lisa was quite capable of arguing with change in a phone box.

"Is there something going on with you and this Janice? You see, what I don't get is that the very first time I met your mum, she called me Janice didn't she, and you looked at her in panic. I didn't say anything because I knew about your reputation and so I thought I'd let it go. But now we're a partnership, two people on the road to marriage and I find out that you have a secret *friend* called Janice." She really emphasised the word friend which made me feel quite uncomfortable. The toast wasn't helping either as I could feel myself choking on it.

I reached for the orange juice from the fridge and poured a small glass, knocking it back in one before I put the phone in my pocket and walked towards the door.

"I'm telling you, I'll get to the bottom of this. If I find out that you've been shagging someone behind my back I won't be responsible for my actions."

I did believe her, scarily enough. I was quite sure Lisa would be capable of coming at me with a meat cleaver in my sleep and I knew she wouldn't let this drop. As I drove to work, all I could think about was that I needed to tell her that Terry had booked a table for four at Luciano's on Saturday night.

Chapter Twenty

*A*s was expected, my day at work went by very slowly and every time someone knocked on the office door my stomach turned over with me thinking it might be Lisa for round two. Thankfully, she stayed out of my way and I decided to stay out of hers. I even went to Marks and Spencer's in the precinct for a sandwich rather than Jack's cafe because I couldn't face seeing Billy Brown again. Thoughts of Janice were swimming through my mind but all for the wrong reasons. Too big a part of me missed her yet I knew I needed to delete her number from my phone and stop thinking about how she was. It was none of my business really and as I'd sent the first text message asking after her, it was simply my fault that this mess had started. If only Lisa had been more understanding and believed me when I'd told her we were just friends, but then again, I had cared a great deal about Janice and at one point had hoped we'd have some sort of relationship. It was only because she made it quite clear to me that nothing would stop her emigrating that I decided to jump in with both feet and make a go of it with Lisa. Did that mean Lisa was my second choice, a bit on the side, an after-thought? Oh shit, this was becoming a complete mess and if I were to make Lisa believe me when I told her that Janice was now just a friend, I knew I had to be completely honest with her. It would mean hurting Lisa, of course it would, but we couldn't start married life with secrets hanging over us. That would have worked for the old Gary, but not me as I'd become. I was trying hard to change my ways and being with Lisa had helped me in more ways than I could have imagined.

After work I went to see mum. She always had the answer and I knew she would help me sort out the mess I'd created. I thought about ringing Lisa first, just to let her know I wouldn't be home at the usual time, but then I decided not to bother. What would be the point in having her slam the phone down on me? I doubted she'd have made us a candlelit dinner for two anyway.

"You look pale, son, are you okay?" Mum could sense a mile off that something was wrong. "Do you want a cuppa?"

I nodded and plonked myself on the sofa.

"Do you want to talk about it?" She came in the front room with a hot cup of tea and a Penguin biscuit, then sidled up to me on the sofa.

"It's Lisa, she's really pissed off with me."

"Again?" Talk about hit a guy when he's down.

"Yeah, again. I've cocked up and she won't listen to my explanation."

"You haven't been playing away have you, son?" She pulled away from me and stared into my eyes, concern written on her face.

"No, of course I haven't. I love Lisa."

"Then why's she pissed off with you?"

"Do you remember I had a night out with a girl called Janice, about eight months ago? Just before I got together with Lisa?"

"Yeah, of course I do. I mistook Lisa for her didn't I?"

"Yeah, and she hasn't forgotten either." I rolled my eyes as mum continued to stare at me. "Problem is, I sent Janice a text the other day. She moved to Australia a couple of months ago and I thought I'd just send her a quick text to ask how she was. It was all very innocent."

"So why's Lisa angry with you then? What have you done?" My mum obviously still had little faith in me.

"I've done nothing, mum, honestly. It was a quick text, nice and brief, just asking after a mate. Only thing is she fired me one back last night after I'd gone to bed and even though she hasn't made it look like we're having it off or anything, she said she misses me and keeps thinking about what we could have had."

"Well that all seems quite innocent to me. Have you explained to Lisa that she's an ex-girlfriend and now you're just friends? I don't believe Lisa doesn't trust you. You're supposed to be getting married for heaven's sake."

"I didn't tell Lisa about Janice you see, and now she thinks I've been keeping Janice a secret all this time. I told her we went out on a date but it didn't work out and she says she remembers you calling her Janice by mistake so I guess she's put two and two together and made five. Shit mum, what am I going to do? I really do love Lisa and I don't want us to split up over this."

"Well, you should get your sorry arse around there and tell the girl exactly what you're telling me. Lisa's a decent sort, she thinks the world of you. And from the sounds of it her parents are decent people, too. You could do a hell of a lot worse." Mum stood up and folded her arms, a stern look on her face. I'd pissed off the two main women in my life in one day. It couldn't get much worse than that.

"I'll finish my tea then I'll go and talk to her."

"You need to delete Janice from your contacts list as well and show Lisa what you've done. Grovel, beg and make her see that she's wrong for doubting you. Blimey, it's your birthday on Saturday and Terry's splashing out on a meal for us all. You need to sort things out before then."

I didn't believe what I was hearing. "I couldn't give a shit about Terry splashing out at Luciano's. I think my impending marriage is more important than a fucking ham and pineapple pizza."

"Watch your language." She whacked me over the head and I ducked.

"Sorry, but come on, mum. I think we might need to give this weekend a miss. Lisa and I need to get this sorted and we're not going to do that with you and Terry making eyes at each other."

"Terry's a good man, and a generous one at that. And what's more, he's asked me again if I'll move in with him and I've said yes. I had the house valued yesterday. I wasn't going to tell you, not yet anyway, but you might as well know. If you wanted to buy it before I put it on the market then I'm giving you first refusal and Terry and I are going to give you money for a decent deposit as a wedding present." She looked through the window and started tapping her foot. She hadn't done that since dad left.

I stood up and put my arms around her. "I don't know what to say, mum. That's amazing."

"You need to speak to Lisa and sort this out quickly because I think Terry was hoping for an answer on Saturday night. He talked about us having champagne at the meal to celebrate because he was sure you'd agree."

"I do agree. I can't thank you both enough. But I do need to talk to Lisa. Do you think Terry would mind if we postponed going out on Saturday and made it next weekend instead?"

"I'm not sure what I'll tell him because if I tell him you and Lisa are having problems I imagine he'll be a bit reluctant to be handing over cheques for a wedding present, don't you?" As usual, she had a point.

"Okay, please let me speak to Lisa and I'll ring you tomorrow." She nodded and squeezed me like she used to do when I was a little boy.

"Go home, Gary. Make this work with you and Lisa. Delete that girl's number off your phone and forget about her. You need to move on and leave all traces of your colourful past behind you, for the sake of your impending marriage." She kissed my cheek then pulled away. "Ring me tomorrow, son."

I walked to the front door and opened it before turning around to face her. "Thanks, mum. I love you."

"I love you too, darling."

Now I had the job of convincing Lisa that I loved her, too.

❦

When I drew up outside the house, I noticed Lisa hovering at the front bedroom window then dart behind the curtains when she obviously saw my car. Good, she'd been waiting for me to come home, I thought. At least that must mean she wondered where I was and maybe even *cared* where I was. I locked the car up then went inside the house, leaving my briefcase in the hall.

"Where've you been?" She was stood at the top of the stairs, hand on the banister rail and her other hand by her side.

I looked up at her. "I called in to see my mum." I went into the front room and heard her clomp downstairs.

"We need to talk." Her voice was firm and it sent shivers down my spine. I sat down on the armchair not wanting her to think I'd assumed she'd forgiven me by sitting on the sofa and waiting for her to join me.

"Yeah, we do. There's nothing going on with Janice.

There never has been. She's a mate, and I'll never see her again because she now lives in Sydney."

"I believe you." Thank fuck for that. Now we could move on with the making up part. I was just going to get up from the chair and join her on the sofa when she continued. "The thing is you must have been seeing her at some point because your mum called me Janice by mistake and that tells me you were most probably two-timing me. Am I right?"

Breathe, Gary, breathe. I needed to tell her the truth if we were to move on from this.

"Right, I'm being completely honest with you now so don't start freaking out. It was nothing against you, or her, but I'd arranged a night out with her before you came onto me and I thought I'd just carry on with the planned date. I know it was wrong and I should have said no to her, or even no to you, but I didn't. I'm sorry for that but it's a long time ago and it really was only one date. After you and me got together I didn't see Janice again, I swear to you." She had to believe me now, my face alone must have been a picture of innocence.

"Okay, I accept that. And I also accept that you wanted to keep your options open. I don't blame you for doing that though I wish you had told me you were going out with someone else." Lisa was looking pensive now. She shook her head. "But I can't understand why you needed to keep in touch with her. Why did you send her a text to see how she is? She's not in your life anymore and if what you're telling me is the truth, then she never really was. So why?"

I took my mobile phone out of my trouser pocket and switched it on. It buzzed into life before emitting the usual crap tune. The alert bell rang for text messages and my stomach flipped as I opened the folder, praying there were none from Janice. Thankfully there weren't. It was my mum wishing me luck and Alfie telling me about a band called Parade who were playing at Banana's in a couple of weeks and did I want to go on a lad's night out with him. I decided to ignore that one. I pressed the 'contacts' button and scrolled down to Janice's name.

"Look," I said, showing Lisa the phone. "I'm deleting her from my contacts." I pressed the delete button, swallowing as I realised I was cutting all traces of Janice from my life. "She means nothing to me. Not now, not ever."

"But she did, didn't she?" Lisa stared straight into my eyes.

I looked at her and sighed. "Yeah, okay, she did, but only for a short time. I thought we had a good thing going but then she announced she was emigrating and I knew there was no point in pursuing a relationship with her."

"So you decided to give me a go instead. Is that right?"

"It wasn't like that, Lisa. You're making me out to be some kind of gigolo. I'd fancied you for ages and you know that, otherwise I wouldn't have arranged to go out with you would I. Like you said, I was keeping my options open and I know that was wrong and I can't apologise enough, I really can't. I never thought you'd be hurt. From that first time we slept together I knew it was you I wanted. You have to believe that, babe."

"A part of me really wants to believe you. But I'm not used to being someone's second choice and that's what I was to you. If Janice hadn't been emigrating you'd have stayed with her and probably wouldn't have gone out with me at all." She walked to the window and looked onto the street. "Or would you? Would you have two-timed us both, is that what you planned to do?"

I stood up and joined her at the window, putting my arm around her waist. "Of course it's not what I planned to do. Lisa, I love you, we're planning a future together.

Isn't that more important than a daft text from Janice?"

"It's not just the text though, or the fact you conveniently didn't tell me about your friend Janice." She emphasised the friend-word again. "It's the thoughts I now have that I was your second choice and she was your first, and because you couldn't have her, you settled for me, which makes me second best. I don't want to be second best to you. I want to be the woman you'll do anything for, the woman you'll go to the moon for. And now I just feel as though I'm kidding myself."

"I can't believe you feel like this, sweetheart. You were never second choice and you're certainly not second best. You're my fiancée, my wife-to-be, my future." I realised I was starting to sound a little too cheesy as Lisa turned to face me with raised eyebrows. "You might even be the mother of my children one day."

She pulled away from me and went in to the kitchen where she reached for a glass and filled it with tap water.

"Come on, Lisa, stop this. What happened with Janice is in the past, it isn't important. It's never been important, not really. What *we* have is special. It's so much more than I've ever had with anyone, and I think you feel the same way, don't you?" I stood close up behind her as she looked through the kitchen window onto the back garden. Then she suddenly turned around and stared at me, a look of anxiety appearing in her eyes.

"I'm pregnant, Gary."

Hmm, I thought, pregnant, that's another term for 'having a baby'. No, I must have misheard. I don't understand what she's saying.

"What do you mean, you're pregnant?" I asked, as tears began streaming down her face.

"We're having a baby." She put her hand on her

stomach and tried a weak smile, looking at me as though I was thick.

"A baby?"

"Yes, a baby. That's what pregnant means."

"You're pregnant?"

She nodded but the smile faded and the tears continued to fall. She stepped away from me, alarm written all over her face.

"Oh god, please don't do this."

"Do what?"

She gestured with her hands. "This. This silly male reaction, as though it's not yours or something. As though you don't understand how I could have got pregnant."

"I'm not doing anything." I hesitated for a moment. "But how *did* you get pregnant?"

"Don't you want this? I've been scared to death of telling you all week. Please just tell me you're okay with this..."

"Scared to tell me?" To Lisa, I must have sounded like I'd just been beamed down from Mars. I was struggling to take in her news.

"Okay," she said, turning and walking towards the kitchen door. "I'll leave you alone for a while to get your head around it."

"No, wait," I shouted after her. "We're having a baby? Me and you?" I looked at her stomach area. "You mean my baby is growing in there?"

"Yes, Gary. That's exactly what I mean."

The news was starting to sink in, whether it was looking at her stomach that did it I don't know, but all I could see was the image of a tiny baby growing inside Lisa, my tiny baby, ours. I didn't know whether to laugh or cry. So I did both.

She ran to me and flung her arms around my neck. "Are you happy about it?"

"Yes," I hiccupped, through snot and tears. "Yes,

fuck, yes. We're going to be a mummy and daddy." I pulled away and put my hand on Lisa's stomach as though expecting to feel movement. "How far gone are you?"

"About eight weeks. I did the test on Tuesday night."

I thought back to Tuesday night. It was the last time we'd made love before she stormed off after I'd had the balls to complain about things moving too quickly. Looking back in hindsight, it wasn't surprising Lisa was pissed off with me after I'd said that.

"Why didn't you tell me sooner?"

"I was going to tell you on Wednesday night but after all that shit with your ex girlfriend I couldn't be arsed. Then I just didn't know what to do."

I hugged her. "All that shit with Janice is well and truly behind us. You do realise that, don't you?"

"Yes, I do now. But I need to know you want this baby. As we haven't set an official wedding date yet I thought we could perhaps make it soon, before I start putting weight on. At least that way I'll fit into the dress I've bought."

I pulled away again. This needed thinking about. She'd just landed the bombshell of pregnancy and now she wanted us to set a wedding date in the very near future. Thinking time was needed, and so was a strong drink. I reached for the bourbon out of the drinks cabinet and poured a large glass, knocking it back in one. Not my best move considering Lisa was standing waiting for my reaction.

"I'll take that as you not wanting to marry me now, shall I?" She had her arms folded again. I hoped I wasn't going to have put up with seven more months of this arms-folding business because I was already sick of it. My mum was the expert in arms-folding and stern looks; the last thing I wanted was to have Lisa take her place.

"Of course I want to marry you. More than ever. I just don't know whether we should hang fire, just until the baby's born." I poured another drink.

"That won't help," Lisa said, looking at my glass of bourbon.

I looked at it also. "No, you're right." I put the glass on the sideboard and went into the front room, sitting down in the arm chair.

"Look, I know this is a shock. I'm shocked as well. You know I was on the pill and for some reason it's failed. But we were going to have kids one day and now is as good a time as any. We can talk about the wedding date another time if you like."

But we both knew it needed discussing as soon as possible. I shook my head. "No, I think it'd be good to get married soon, if that's what you really want." Maybe now was the right time to tell Lisa we were going out with mum and Terry tomorrow night. I cleared my throat and gave her the news.

"That sounds nice. We'll be able to make our announcement won't we, two celebrations together."

"Well, err, yeah, I suppose so."

"I wish you'd sound more enthusiastic about it."

I moved to the sofa and sat next to her. She seemed frail somehow, as though she'd lost weight. I put my arm around her shoulder and pulled her into me. "I'm absolutely thrilled, honestly. It's just such a lot to take in. Let's tell mum about the baby first then think about wedding dates maybe next week. What do you think?"

Lisa snuggled into me. I'd finally cracked it. "Okay, I'm happy to do that. I guess your mum will need to get used to being a grandmother."

"Have you told your mum and dad yet?"

"No, of course I haven't. I wanted you to be the first to know. Maybe we can tell them tomorrow morning. I'll ring them."

At least Lisa was speaking to me again. The

atmosphere was so much nicer when she was happy. I didn't sleep much that night though, and every time I did nod off I dreamt about giant babies and duvet covers that turned into nappies, of which I had the job of changing.

Chapter Twenty-One

*L*isa's mum and dad were thrilled to hear they were going to be grandparents, which relieved me I can tell you. I was dreading what her dad might say and I wasn't absolutely sure her mum would approve of a baby before we were married. But Lisa also told them that we'd most likely bring the wedding forward and arrange it within the next month before she started showing. I still wasn't sure that was what I wanted but I also knew that Lisa would never have forgiven me if we'd waited until after the birth and she struggled to lose her baby weight. She was very conscious of her appearance and her slim figure. I just envied the baby who was going to have free reign on those nipples every hour of the day.

We got dressed up for our night out and met mum and Terry at the restaurant at eight o'clock. They were already seated and a waiter led us to the table where Terry stood up and shook my hand, then gave Lisa a little peck on both cheeks. I kissed mum and Lisa did the same before we sat down. The waiter handed us a menu each and took our drink's order. Fortunately, I don't think they recognised me from the last time I'd been in and scrimped with the tip.

"Happy Birthday, son," mum sang, much to my embarrassment. "Have you had a nice day?"

"Fabulous," I grinned, holding Lisa's hand under the table. Lisa squeezed my hand and lifted her glass.

"Happy Birthday, honey," she said, as the others joined in.

"Gary," mum leaned over towards me and whispered in my ear. "Did you talk it through with Lisa?"

I looked at her, puzzled.

"You know, the deposit money, you buying my house?"

Oh fuck. I'd completely forgotten after all the excitement of the baby news. How the hell had I forgotten to mention that? Now I'd look a right prick as I just landed this on her without any warning. Terry was studying the menu, as was Lisa.

"I haven't told her yet, I forgot," I whispered.

Mum leant back in her chair and sighed, then she looked at Lisa. "Gary has something to tell you, love. He should have told you on Thursday night and I've no idea why he didn't." She glared at me and pulled a face. She might as well have just called me an arsehole and be done with it.

"Yeah, err, with everything that's happened I forgot to tell you about mum and Terry's generous offer."

"What generous offer?" Lisa asked, closing the menu and putting it on the table.

"They want to give us a deposit as a wedding present to put down on a house." I paused. "Mum's house, to be precise."

It was a miracle that Lisa didn't knock everything over when she jumped up and dived on me. "Oh my god, that's amazing." She ran to mum and hugged her. "Thank you, Christine, thank you so much." Then Terry got the treatment. "I don't know what to say. This is incredibly kind of you both." Then I got the treatment again. "You know what this means don't you, Gary? We can move before..." I stopped her quickly. I didn't want mum to find out in a burst of excitement that she was going to be a grandmother.

"Before what?" mum asked, not missing a trick.

Lisa sat down and ran her hands over her stomach. "You tell them."

I looked at mum who was now watching Lisa caressing herself.

"Mum, Lisa's pregnant. We only found out the other night. You're going to be a grandma."

Mum's eyes lit up as a smile appeared and her whole face seemed to beam at me, then she stood up and gave me the Lisa treatment, flinging her arms around me and kissing me all over my face, in the middle of the restaurant.

"Think this is cause for a triple celebration," Terry said, signalling to the waiter and ordering a bottle of their finest champagne. All I could think was that the man must be loaded.

"How far gone are you; when's it due; how do you feel; have you got any cravings yet?" I got the impression mum was thrilled.

"We're so excited, aren't we?" Lisa held my hand, raised it to her mouth and kissed it.

"Absolutely chuffed to bits," I replied.

"What about the wedding?" mum asked.

"Well, we think we might bring it forward and get married before I get too fat." Lisa rubbed her stomach again.

"I think that's a great idea," mum said. I knew at that point I didn't stand a chance and my opinion about our forthcoming wedding would matter not one jot.

Terry looked at me, a sympathetic expression on his face. "Looks like the two women in your life will have a lot to talk about over the next few months." He took the champagne from the bucket and poured it into the four flutes.

"Only a tiny drop for me," Lisa said, putting her hand over the glass.

"To Gary, Lisa and the little one," Terry said, raising his glass. What a nice guy, I thought. Mum could have done a lot worse. Age gap or not, he was quickly growing on me and the fact he was loaded meant I wouldn't have to worry too much about mum once she'd moved out of her house and into his.

The night went swimmingly, though once again there could have been more food on the plates. However, Terry paid the bill without a flinch whilst we all tried to avoid looking at it, and then the waiter led us to the coat stand and held out mum and Lisa's coats whilst they slipped into them. It had gone really well and at last things seemed to be looking better for Lisa and me.

We spent most of Sunday in bed whilst Lisa gave me lots of birthday presents, all of which didn't cost any money. I'd invited Jez and Angela round that night, and mentioned it to Alfie if he was interested but I suspected he wouldn't turn up. I hadn't seen or heard much from him for ages now and even though a part of me was a bit sad that our close friendship seemed to be fading away, I was quite disappointed that he wasn't happy for me, or at least didn't act as though he was. It had been the previous weekend when I'd asked him to come over for a few drinks, just because it was my birthday, as obviously, last weekend we didn't know about the baby, the new home or bringing the wedding forward.

"Not sure I can make it," he'd responded when I'd asked.

"Oh, right. Well, the invite's there if you can. You're welcome to bring a bird if you like."

"I'm off birds right now, Gaz. If I come I'll be on my own."

"Everything going well at work?" I asked, trying hard to make some sort of conversation.

"Nah, it's shite. Fucking Graham, the tosser in charge of my department is threatening sackings and he's giving me a hard time at the moment so I'm keeping my head down."

"You'll be alright, Alfie. You're a valued member of staff. Don't forget, they head-hunted you."

"It makes no difference these days. If the money isn't there to pay wages they just tell you to fuck off." Alfie was in one of his 'no one can talk to me' moods so I gave in and called an end to the phone call. I wanted to feel sorry for him but he was a law unto himself. He'd never listened to anyone in his life, even though he'd landed himself a great job at Peterson Blare, an accountancy firm in Bedworth. The problem with Alfie was he thought he knew it all, thought he always had one up on everyone else and that's where he often got caught out, especially where Jez was concerned, and now me. I knew Jez wouldn't let him drag him down and I certainly wasn't going to.

Jez and Angela arrived at half-past seven with a bottle of wine and four cans of Fosters. Angela gave me a little peck on the cheek then handed me a box of Thornton's Continental.

"Happy Birthday, Gary," she said, before going into the kitchen to join Lisa.

"Come through," I said to Jez, taking the cans from him.

"You seem at home here, mate," he said. "It's looking good." Jez had changed since he'd met Angela. He seemed calmer somehow, more refined.

"Yeah, but we won't be staying here." I opened a can

and took a gulp. "We're buying mum's place. She and Terry are giving us the deposit for a wedding present. Probably be moving in the next few months."

"Blimey, you're not hanging around are you?! What's going on, she up the duff?" Jez laughed loudly and sank back into the sofa. Then he looked at me, taking the can away from his face, obviously noticing that I wasn't laughing. "Never? Is Lisa pregnant?"

"Keep it down, mate. We weren't going to tell anyone yet. She's only a couple of months gone. We wanted to wait till she was three months."

"Fuck me, mate. I'm thrilled for you. Why wait to tell everyone? You're going to be a dad."

"I know, but Lisa's a bit worried about losing it. They reckon there's more chance of having a miscarriage within the first three months, that's why we don't want to tell anyone yet."

"You've told your mum though?"

"Yeah, told her last night and she's chuffed to bits. Lisa's mum and dad are too. Just keep it to yourself for now though, eh? We're not telling anyone at work or any other friends for a few weeks."

"No worries, mate. I won't tell a soul." He made a cross symbol against his chest. "But seriously, mate, this is awesome news. I'm really pleased for you." He hit his can against mine, splashing lager onto the carpet. I quickly rubbed it off before Lisa would notice.

"What's going on in here then?" Lisa and Angela joined us in the front room, standing at the door and grinning like two Cheshire cats.

"Just wishing Gary a happy birthday." Jez looked at me and winked.

"You honestly think I've come over with the last shower, don't you Gary Stringer?" Lisa came over to me and squeezed my head. "It's okay, I've told Angela about the baby and she's promised not to tell anyone, not yet anyway."

Jez stood up and went towards Lisa. "I'm really happy for you both," he said, kissing her on the cheek. "You'll make fantastic parents."

Lisa squeezed me again. "Yeah, I reckon we will," she grinned.

By ten o'clock we'd got through a bottle of wine, eight cans of Fosters and a carton of orange juice that Lisa was drinking. We started on a game of charades but half an hour in Lisa was feeling knackered and so Jez kindly stood up and announced they'd be going. We had work the following day anyway so it was for the best.

"Sorry Alfie didn't come, mate," Jez said as they were putting their coats on. "I don't know what's wrong with him lately. It's like he's jealous of us."

"Is he seeing anyone?" I asked. "Only when I invited him round tonight I said he could bring a bird with him and he said he's off women."

"As far as I know he's been seeing someone at work but I think she's married so maybe she's decided to give it a go with her old man. I honestly haven't spoken to him for ages now and he doesn't seem to be in much either."

"Oh well, suppose I'd better go round and see him soon, tell him about the wedding and all that. I want him to come of course."

"I'll let you know this week when he's in." Jez shook my hand. "Seriously, mate, I'm happy for you. It's been a great night." He ushered Angela through the door and they started walking down the street. It was a good half an hour's walk back to Jez's apartment but they didn't seem bothered. Lisa had offered to run them home, but they said they preferred to walk and get the fresh air.

"Well that went well," Lisa said, turning off the lamps in the front room before following me upstairs. "We've had a great laugh."

"What would you think if I asked Jez to be my best man?" I went into our bedroom and started stripping off.

"I think that's a great idea. I might ask Angela if she wants to be a bridesmaid. What about Alfie though, won't he be offended if you don't ask him?"

"I don't think Alfie will even want to come to the wedding. From what Jez is telling me, he's jealous of us. Seems he's unhappy right now and won't talk to anyone. Thought I might go and see him next week and ask him to be an usher, but I'll see what he says first about the wedding."

"Are you going to tell him about the baby?"

"No, not yet. I've asked Jez not to say anything as well."

"I hope he won't be upset. I don't like the thought of you losing a good friend. I wonder if it's me."

"What do you mean?" I got into bed and pulled the duvet back for Lisa.

She climbed in beside me, dressed in fluffy pyjamas that told me sex was off the cards. "Well, it just feels as though since you and I got together he's kept out of your way. Maybe he thinks you're under the thumb of something."

"He most probably does, but who gives a shit. He can think what he likes. I've moved on I'm done with that lifestyle, Lisa, and the sooner he realises that the better."

She snuggled against my chest. "I love you. You're the best thing that's ever happened to me." She lifted her head up and kissed me softly on my lips, sending a shiver down my spine and a rush of blood to my cock. "Down, boy," Lisa laughed, as she patted it gently, then snuggled up again and went to sleep.

Jez rang my mobile on Wednesday night to tell me Alfie had just arrived home and he heard him closing his front door. I asked if he'd got anyone with him but Jez said not. So I grabbed my car keys, gave Lisa a quick kiss and headed out the door. I arrived at the apartment block ten minutes later, having driven like a lunatic to avoid missing Alfie again. He answered the intercom and sighed when he heard my voice, then clicked the door open.

I went into the apartment and found him slumped on the sofa watching Emmerdale. I don't think I'd ever known Alfie to watch Emmerdale. I sat on the chair nearby and put a couple of cans on the coffee table which was strewn with newspapers and car magazines.

"What's going on, Alfie?" I asked, snapping the ring pull.

"If you've come here to have a go at me then fuck off."

"I haven't come here to have a go at you, mate, I'm just concerned about you. Haven't seen you for weeks and when I do see you you're distant and unfriendly."

"Been let out have you?" he mocked, picking up a can.

"Are you jealous of me and Lisa?"

"No, I'm not fucking jealous. Get over yourself, you tosser."

"Are you jealous of Jez and Angela then?"

"Oh, just do one, Gary, I've got enough on my plate without your bollocking lectures." He took a large gulp of the beer and sank back into the sofa.

"You're a good mate, Alfie, always have been. You, me and Jez, we're a team. We tell each other everything." Alfie shrugged and I moved to stand up, wondering if there was any point in me staying. "I'll be there when you want to talk, mate. And in the meantime, I want you as an usher at my wedding. Lisa and I are tying the knot in about a month's time and I want you there to support me."

Alfie looked up at me as I stood over him. I was

shocked when I saw he'd got tears in his eyes and it prompted me to kneel at his side and ask again what the matter was.

"I'm scared, Gaz. Fucking freaked out."

"What are you scared of, mate?"

He started shuffling on the sofa then rubbed his hand against his thigh. "I've got a lump on me bits. Fucking massive it is. Was shagging this bird a few weeks ago and she found it. I'd noticed it before but hadn't wanted to think about it. But she's a nurse and reckons I need to get it checked out pronto."

"Shit, mate. Have you had it checked out then?"

"No. Fucking hate doctors, they're bastards."

"Don't talk like that, mate. They're not bastards. They'll help you and if it's serious they'll sort it out for you. We pay into a health service, Alfie, you need to get your money's worth." I smiled at him weakly, hoping it might prompt him to smile back. Thankfully he did.

"I know, but doctors terrify me. After my mum and dad died I said I'd never see a doctor ever again. I spent days in that hospital running from one bed to another and none of the doctors could save them."

"They had massive injuries, Alfie. You know that. They told you from the start that it would be a miracle if they survived. You saw the state of the car, mate, you saw it."

"Yeah, I did, but I was eighteen, Gaz. Eighteen. Fuck me, man. I was an orphan, they never saw me leave college and get a job, and they've never seen this place. I had to fend for myself as soon as I became an adult and it was fucking hard, mate."

I remembered it well, Nettie and Colin Black, hit by another car head on as the driver was overtaking a string of lorries on a B road in Devon. The driver was pronounced dead at the scene but Alfie's mum and dad were airlifted to the local hospital where they underwent emergency surgery then kept on a life support machine until Alfie could get to them. But after a few days they decided to switch the machines off, knowing they couldn't be saved. It was horrendous and Alfie came to live with me, mum and dad for a few weeks while he got himself together. After that, he moved in with his auntie whilst he finished college and then landed himself the job at Peterson Blare. He'd done well for himself considering what he'd been through but he always had a rebellious streak and I knew there were underlying issues for it. It was obvious to me now that he still found his parents' death difficult to deal with.

"Right, here's the deal," I began. "Get yourself an appointment at the doctors this week and I'll come with you. Ring them first thing, say it's an emergency then ring my mobile and I'll meet you at the surgery."

He looked at me, tears still prevalent in his eyes. "You'd do that for me?" he asked.

"Of course I fucking will, you twat. You and Jez are my best mates, I'd do anything for you, you know that."

And then Alfie did something he'd never done before in all the time I'd known him. He hugged me. I felt a bit awkward at first, hoping he wasn't going to muscle in for a kiss as well, but he pulled away, wiped his tears and took another swig of beer.

"Go and get me another can will you. They're in the fridge."

I'd got my mate back again.

Chapter Twenty-Two

When I got home that night after seeing Alfie, I rang Jez to put him in the picture and made him promise not to tell Alfie that he knew. I assured him I'd keep him in the loop about the doctor's appointment and would try and talk Alfie into opening up to us both, maybe over a pizza at the weekend.

Lisa was asleep when I got in, tucked under the duvet breathing softly. I lay awake for quite some time thinking about how shit Alfie must have been feeling and asking myself if I should have gone to see him sooner. But he was a typical cave-man, didn't open up unless he really had to and I knew that even if I had gone to see him, there would be no guarantee that he'd have told me about the lump.

He rang me on Thursday morning to tell me he had an appointment at the surgery at four o'clock that day but he wanted to go on his own. He asked if I'd take him to the hospital though as he was sure he'd end up there for one reason or another. I let Jez know and he offered to come to the hospital as well.

Unfortunately, the doctor said it was very urgent that he get the lump properly checked as he wasn't sure how serious it was. An appointment for an ultra sound was made for the following week and so I booked the day off work and told Alfie I'd take him. He was grateful, I could tell, though I think he'd been drinking heavily when he rang to tell me.

The following Tuesday, Lisa kissed me on her way out the door and I got myself ready to go and pick Alfie up. Jez was coming with us also, said there was no way he was being left out. Alfie said he'd rather not have all the fuss but as he didn't refuse both of us going with him, I took that as him being glad of the company. We fumbled about for change when we got to the hospital car park then made our way to the correct department, asking a good looking nurse in the corridor to confirm we were on the right route. It was the same hospital Alfie's nurse-friend worked at though he'd since told me it was the uniform he fancied, rather than her.

We left him to it when we arrived at the main desk, whilst he checked himself in and was told to get himself into a hospital gown in the changing room. Jez and I sat in the waiting area and picked up a few magazines, flicking through them absently, trying to pass the time without worrying about Alfie too much. The whole thing didn't take long and Alfie returned to us fully dressed with a solemn look on his face.

"They'll let me know either later today or tomorrow morning." He went towards the door to the toilet. "What if I have to have one of me balls chopped off?" he said, before going inside the Gents.

I looked at Jez and we both shrugged. It was an awful situation to be in and we both felt for him. Memories of his parents were obviously going through Jez's mind as well as my own as Jez asked, "Has he talked about his mum and dad to you recently?"

"He mentioned them the other night when I went to see him, but he doesn't usually talk about them otherwise."

"He's never got over it. I don't think he ever will."

"It's not surprising really is it? The poor guy must have gone through hell and back. And now he feels like he's there again, only this time it's his own body that he thinks is failing."

Jez nodded and we both watched as the Gent's door opened and Alfie came out. He seemed a bit better as we walked back to the car and we decided to stop at McDonald's for a burger on our way home.

"So," Alfie said, munching on a Big Mac. "We never talked about you getting wed. When will it be?"

"Next month," I said. "Lisa's got a cancellation for the 17th of June."

"So how come you've decided to get married in a hurry, or is that a daft question?"

I laughed. "It's a daft question."

"I fucking knew it. Well done, you're not firing blanks after all. Congratulations." He slurped his coke then carried on filling his face with the burger.

"I wasn't going to tell you as she's not at the three month stage yet, but she seems to be sailing through it up to now, not much morning sickness."

"Let me eat this, man!" Alfie choked, coughing up a piece of lettuce and spitting it onto the foot-well in my car.

"I want you to be an usher at the wedding."

"What do I need to do?"

"Give out the order of service, show guests to their seats. There won't be a lot there, I'm trying to keep it fairly low key though Lisa and mum seem to have other ideas, but an usher is a very important role. Are you up for it?"

Alfie wiped his mouth with a napkin. "Yeah, I'll do that. So long as I'm not laid up having a bollock chopped off."

"Don't be daft. It won't come to that. You'll be fine."

"So who's your best man?"

Shit, I hadn't asked Jez and now I knew I'd have to in front of Alfie. He was feeling crap as it was, the last thing I wanted to do was make him feel even worse by letting him think Jez was more of a best mate than he was. It wasn't the case, of course, but we hadn't seen much of Alfie and it just made sense to ask Jez. Plus, after all the events of the last few days, I didn't think Alfie would be up to the job anyway.

I looked at Jez who sat in the front seat next to me. "I was going to ask Jez."

To my surprise, Alfie patted him on the shoulder. "Well done, mate. I think you'll make a cracking best man."

I turned to look at Alfie in the back seat. "Thanks, Alfie. I don't want you to think..."

"Fuck off, Gaz, you don't need me standing lop sided at the altar with only one bollock. Jez is the best man for the job." And with that last remark, we all fell over in our seats laughing at Alfie's sense of humour.

❦

The following day, Alfie rang me at work to tell me the good news. It was a cyst. It would have to be removed but it wasn't as urgent as it would have been should it have been cancerous. I was thrilled for Alfie and thought I heard his voice quivering on the phone, but I told him I'd take him back to the hospital for the operation when the appointment came through, and if I wasn't able to because I was on my honeymoon or something, then Jez would do it. One way or another, he wouldn't have to go through it on his own. I was just grateful I had my two best mates back and we could once again call ourselves the troublesome three even if we weren't quite so troublesome anymore.

The wedding plans were finalised and everything was in place. We'd chosen our wedding rings and I'd booked us a week in the South of France. Mine, Jez and Alfie's suits were ordered, and Angela's bridesmaid dress was ready to collect. Mum had organised the church and the flowers and Lisa's mum had arranged the buffet, disco and the wedding breakfast. We had fifty guests, most of whom were Lisa's family, but invited a further seventy-five to the disco in the evening. My idea of low key had well and truly been blown.

The house was going through as well. I'd managed to secure a mortgage and Terry had written a cheque for the deposit. Mum kept bringing boxes home from work to pack up her stuff and gave me loads for Lisa's belongings too. I still had unpacked boxes which were piled up in Lisa's spare bedroom. It was all coming together. A new future awaited us, a baby on the way, new house and a life I only once dreamt of. But it was happening. I'd still wake up in the morning and wonder if I'd imagined Lisa in my life, if being a dad was just something that happened to other men. But no, there she was, beautiful and glowing and thoroughly enjoying being pregnant with our baby.

The week before the wedding I popped into the precinct for lunch, boycotting Jack's cafe as usual and heading straight for Marks and Spencer's. I bought a cheese and ham sandwich for Lisa and a chicken and mayo for me, then grabbed two bottles of diet coke from the fridge. I stood in the queue and watched as the young lad at the till was struggling to scan a bar code. As I shuffled about from one foot to the other, I saw a figure in the corner of my eye, a woman who looked familiar, and I swivelled, nearly knocking into the guy behind me as I tried to get a better view of her. Then it hit me as though someone had punched me with a baseball bat in the stomach. It was Janice.

Her hair was a different shade and she was tanned, standing holding a basket of food and studying the ready meals shelf. I paid for my items then walked away from the tills, turning around again to see if it really was her and not just a figment of my imagination. It was, and she was now looking straight at me.

Oh fuck, I thought, she's seen me. And then she started walking towards me, a smile etched on her face. I didn't know whether to run or hide amongst the fresh fruit and veg that I was now standing close to. With the veg in one direction and Janice in the other I knew there was no escape, and all the time I was thinking about Lisa and the fact she'd probably be wondering where I was with her sandwich.

"Hi, fancy seeing you in here." Janice said, approaching me.

"Hi there. How come you're back home?"

"I'm just visiting for a while. It's mum and dad's pearl wedding anniversary next week so I came back to surprise them."

"Pearl? How long is that?"

"Thirty years," she answered. "So, how are you?"

"Yeah, I'm good thanks. Just popped out for a bite to eat."

"Don't you go in Jack's anymore?" She glanced at the green plastic bag I was holding containing mine and Lisa's lunch.

"I've been in once or twice but I tend to make my lunch these days as don't have much time to get out anymore."

"How's your job going?"

"It's great, I'm really enjoying it." It was small talk. She knew it, I knew it. "How's it going in Oz?"

"Yeah, it's great, I absolutely love it."

"You look well, great tan." I smiled and she smiled back, that beautiful, familiar expression as her face lit up.

"So, what you up to these days?" she asked, putting her basket on the floor.

"Oh, you know, nothing much." Nothing much? What the fuck was I saying?!

"Still with your girlfriend?"

"Well, err, yeah, you could say that."

"Oh, have you decided to settle down at long last?" she smirked.

"I'm getting married on Saturday." She lifted her eyebrows and seemed to gaze straight through me.

"Wow!" It seemed to be the only word she could muster up.

"She's pregnant."

"Fuck." Janice laughed then. "Oh heck, I didn't mean to say that, listen to me, I never used to swear like that before I moved to Sydney. Well, I'm pleased for you. A baby and a wife, wow...gosh...I mean, yeah, really pleased for you."

"Anyway," I said, turning my body slightly and signalling towards the door. "I need to get back, got lunch to eat before the afternoon starts."

Janice picked up her basket. "Of course, I don't want to keep you." She leant towards me and gave me a little peck on the cheek. "Congratulations. Hope everything goes well for you."

"Thanks. You take care and, err, see you around maybe." Janice turned on her heels and strolled off. I suspected there and then that I'd never see her again.

I spent the rest of that afternoon thinking about Janice and wondering if I'd bump into her again before she went back to Australia. Lisa came in the office at home time and asked if I was ready, but must have noticed a distant expression on my face because she also asked if I was okay. I assured her I was, put my coat on, picked up my briefcase, gave her a kiss on the lips then ushered her through the door. There were only two days to go until she would become my wife and I needed to start concentrating and make damn sure I'd got Janice well and truly out of my mind and out of my life.

Chapter Twenty-Three

*L*isa's mum and dad arrived on Friday afternoon and we drove them to my mum's where they would be staying for the weekend. Mum had cleaned the house top to bottom until it resembled a show home and she'd arranged to stay at Terry's to give Philip and Margie some privacy and the house to themselves. Mum and Terry were taking Lisa and her parents to Luciano's whilst Jez, Alfie and me were off for a night on the town.

Alfie's appointment for the removal of his cyst wasn't for another month so he was quite relieved that it hadn't seemed as urgent as the doctor first suspected. But he was worried about it and both Jez and I promised we'd be there for him at the hospital and to look after him when he came home. Jez had arranged to have him stay there with him, and Angela kindly offered to nurse him back to health as he recuperated, though I pointed out to Angela that if she wore a nurse's outfit she'd be asking for trouble.

We went in the George and Dragon first where my

dad was waiting for us with a round of drinks. I'd asked him to the wedding but he offered to take me and Lisa out after the honeymoon instead, saying it would have been awkward with mum and Terry there and him showing his girlfriend off. Our next stop was the White Horse where Bethany Calder and her brick-shit-house boyfriend were sat at the bar talking to Bethany's mum. It was like I'd gone back nearly twelve months when I was still a jack-the-lad, not a care in the world, obsessed only with adding another notch to my bedpost. I noticed an engagement ring on Bethany's finger and congratulated them both, telling them I was on my stag night. It wasn't an official stag night of course, Lisa and I had decided that because of the baby we wouldn't do the traditional piss-ups where I got lashed and naked and ended up licking squirty cream off some tart's tits, and she wouldn't do the L-plates and the head veil with a group of girls parading around town making themselves available to anything with a dick. We kept it low-key, and this night out with the lads was one I'd looked forward to ever since Jez had suggested it.

Alfie wanted to go to Benidorm for a week but I refused. After he'd called me a boring bastard and pointed out that I was well and truly under the thumb, I turned to Jez and asked what he wanted to do. Fortunately, he said just a night on the town would be enough and it should be me who made the final decision. I wasn't ruling out a week in Benidorm some other time though, like after the baby had been born and I'd be desperate to get away from dirty nappies, sleepless nights and a hormonal wife.

After receiving a peck on the cheek from Bethany and her mum and a look that was more than capable of killing me from Bethany's brick-shit-house boyfriend, we left the White Horse and carried onto Banana's where the music was thumping. It was an 80s disco night and most people in the club seemed to be dressed up in odd-looking attire; some of the guys even had long wigs on and their faces painted. Adam Ant they weren't, though it was a good atmosphere. Jez found us a table whilst Alfie went to the bar and ordered Jager Bombs all round. The place was pretty packed and there were a few people I knew from college, unfortunately far too many students. It was always the case though and in some ways it made me feel more in tune with them. There had never been a 'them' and 'us' type atmosphere when I'd been around the students and I think they respected me for that. A few girls were jiggling about on the dance floor, thrusting themselves at a group of lads who reminded me very much of me, Alfie and Jez when we were just starting out. I watched as the girls flirted and the boys looked on with admiration, no doubt thinking their luck was in. A part of me missed those days when I had no responsibilities, no need to make a commitment; when I could take a girl back to my place, shag her senseless then close the front door quietly as she left in the early hours of the morning. I went through condoms like Alex Ferguson went through chewing gum back then and would get a hard on if I thought a bird had a packet of three in her handbag.

Alfie came back with a tray of drinks and plonked them on the table. Jez passed me a Jager Bomb, took one for himself and we watched as Alfie picked up his, then we all knocked them back in one. I wasn't sure I wanted another as I'd promised Lisa I'd be on top form and wouldn't be hungover on our wedding day and I knew she'd tell if I was suffering just a little bit. She had a knack of being able to tell what I'd been drinking, never mind *whether* I'd been drinking. I didn't want to upset her on our special day. I guessed Alfie had other ideas and had a feeling he was trying to get me paralytic, but I'd already asked Jez to keep his eye on the situation. Besides, Alfie was on medication for his cyst as it had been giving him jip recently and so we were looking out for him, too.

Two shots later and a few more bottles of Budweiser and I looked at my watch seeing it was eleven-thirty. I was tipsy and determined not to drink anymore for fear of pissing Lisa off. Fortunately, Alfie was being sensible for once and agreed that another drink would be a daft idea as he was already feeling quite drunk. Jez suggested a curry to sober us up and we all piled into The Curry House, where we used to finish our Friday nights out, unless of course we'd found ourselves a notch and were eager to get them home.

It was almost one o'clock by the time we left and we made our way to the taxi rank. I could have done with the walk back to be honest but Jez had promised Lisa that he'd get me back to his place safely and had agreed to take me there in the back of a taxi. I thought he was taking his best-man duties a little too far but at the same time he was being a good friend. If only we'd come out of the curry house five minutes later we wouldn't have seen Janice and her friend Alison walking towards us in the direction of Banana's.

She stopped when she saw us. "Gary, we need to stop meeting like this," she said, smiling and rolling her eyes at the same time. Her friend was giving Alfie the eye, and Alfie was certainly not backing away.

"Hello, Janice," I said, taking my hand off the cab door. "Thought you'd have gone back to Australia by now."

"I've got my ticket booked for next week so I'm making the most of it with Alison." She turned to look at her friend. "We don't see much of each other anymore." Alison tore her eyes away from Alfie for a second whilst she looked at me and smiled. "Alison, this is Gary I was telling you about, from the cafe."

Alison looked me up and down and I wondered if she was related to Billy Brown. "Alright?" she said, before turning back to Alfie.

"We're just on our way home actually. Been having a few drinks with the lads, marking my last night of freedom."

"Oh yes, you're getting married tomorrow aren't you? Are you nervous?" Janice seemed to be teasing me with her eyes, either that or she was coming on to me.

"Not really nervous, just excited," I replied, hoping she'd see I'd moved on.

She moved closer towards me and leant into me, her lips just inches from mine. "It could have been amazing couldn't it?" she said, her eyes flicking from my lips back to my eyes and back to my lips again.

"What could?" I asked, starting to feel a bit shaky.

"You and me," she whispered. "I've missed you so much. I know if I hadn't been going to Sydney you and I could have made a go of it. Even my dad thought I'd change my mind after we got together."

Only we didn't really get together did we, we just had sex and fancied the pants off each other and I was left not knowing if it was Lisa I wanted to be with or if I should try and talk Janice into staying in the UK. I heard Alfie say something to someone as they got into the taxi we were supposed to be going home in and we all stepped aside while it drove away. I looked at him, hoping he'd rescue me from the awkward situation. Alfie was no use, standing chatting to Alison, stroking her silk sleeve.

"Do you want me to give you a minute?" Jez asked, looking from me to Janice.

"Would that be okay? I'd like to talk to you, just to put closure to what happened between us." Closure, I thought, what was this, an American movie?

"I'll go in Lulu's and have a quick half. You've got fifteen minutes, mate." Lulu's was the other nightclub in Bedworth, far too upmarket for the likes of us where drinks were silly prices and birds didn't look at you unless you had a Lamborghini parked outside. I nodded to Jez, mouthing 'thanks' as he turned to walk away.

"We're going in Lulu's as well, Gaz," Alfie said, putting his arm around Alison and leading her down the steps to the main entrance. That left Janice and I standing in the middle of the pavement staring into each other's eyes, not knowing what to say.

"Alone at last..."

"I'm sorry... you first..." Janice started walking slowly and I fell into step beside her.

"I'm getting married tomorrow," I said, making sure Janice definitely knew.

"I'm happy for you, really I am. But can I ask you something?"

"Go ahead." We carried on walking away from the hustle of the night clubs, the taxi rank and the curry houses.

"Are you marrying Lisa because she's pregnant?"

"No, I asked her to marry me before we knew she was pregnant."

"Oh, I see." I detected disappointment in her voice.

"When she realised she was pregnant we decided to bring the wedding forward." I stopped walking. "I would have been happy to wait a while." I have no idea why I said that to Janice. It was like I was trying to make her think I wasn't sure about rushing into marriage with Lisa. She looked up at me.

"If I hadn't been going to Sydney, would we have carried on seeing each other?"

"What do you think?" I couldn't help but notice the red lace of her bra on show and encouraged myself to fix my eyes on hers rather than have my thoughts drifting to what could have been.

"I really liked you, Gary. You made me feel so good about myself. Going to Sydney was something I'd planned a long time ago and I knew I'd always do it one way or another." She shrugged. "I needed to get it out of my system."

"You've settled there now though haven't you?" I asked.

"Yes, I suppose so. I've made friends and been on a date with a guy, but he's not like you. He doesn't make me feel special like you did."

"But it would never have worked, Janice. Long distant relationships seldom do."

She shrugged again, only this time she shivered and I noticed she was feeling cold. I took my jacket off and placed it around her shoulders.

"You always were the gentleman. Lisa's a very lucky girl marrying you. I hope she realises that."

"I'm sure she does," I grinned.

"Can I ask you something else?"

"Go for it."

"If I were to stay here and not go back to Sydney, would there be a chance for us?"

I looked away for a moment. Janice must have known how I felt about her that night I took her back to my place. We'd had sex and it was wonderful, but to me it was so much more. I thought it might have been the start of something special but then I imagined myself falling for someone who just wasn't going to allow herself to get involved due to moving away. There'd have been no point in us having a relationship. She must have known that.

"That's not going to happen though is it?"

"If it were, what would you do?"

"I'm not sure what you're asking me, Janice. I'm getting married tomorrow." I looked at my watch. "Well, today actually."

"Say you weren't getting married and I wasn't going back to Sydney, would there ever have been an 'us'?"

Where was Jez, he said he'd be fifteen minutes. He'd already been gone twenty. I looked around, seeing a few people now queuing at the taxi rank down the street. I couldn't see Jez though and I doubted I'd see Alfie again tonight.

"I fell for you. You knew that didn't you?" Did I, I asked myself. I'd fallen for her but I didn't think she felt the same way. "I couldn't allow myself to get too close to you because I had to pursue this move to Australia. It had all been arranged, mum and dad were thrilled that I was taking the initiative, they were proud of me. If I'd have stayed and cancelled my trip they'd have been disappointed in me."

"No one was asking you to stay," I pointed out, wondering if her intention was to make me feel guilty.

"You could have asked me though," she whispered, her lips almost touching mine now. "I was waiting for you to say you didn't want me to go and I wouldn't have done."

I turned my head, eager to get away. "I didn't think you wanted me to ask you," I said finally, planning my escape from a situation that was in danger of ruining the rest of my life.

All I could think about was Lisa and our unborn baby, how much it would hurt them both. But Janice remained in front of me, her face close to mine. Whether she was waiting for me to kiss her I don't know, but I took a step back, worried she might make a move.

"Come with me next week, let's go to Australia together and start a new life."

"You know I can't do that, Janice." I felt as though I was pleading with her to understand my predicament. What the fuck was I doing talking to Janice in the middle of the pavement, only yards from the centre of Bedworth where people were now clambering out of clubs and pubs, exchanging phone numbers, hailing for taxis, giving good-night kisses to strangers who they'd probably never see again?

"You wanted me once, didn't you?" She was manipulating me. She was also scaring me. I started to wonder what I'd ever seen in her and why I'd felt so moved by her personality when all I was seeing now was a mixed up, jealous woman.

"Yes, I did want you but that was a long time ago, Janice. We've both moved on since then." I started to walk away towards the taxis that were now revving their engines with drunken passengers on board.

Janice hurried beside me, almost running in her high heels to catch me up. "If you're still planning on getting married, make sure you're doing it for the right reasons. You don't have to marry Lisa because she's having your baby. I wouldn't stop you seeing your child."

I stopped and glared at her. She was starting to piss me off. "I'm marrying Lisa because I love her, not because she's having my baby. And I would never leave her, not now. We're going to be a family, a happy family, and I'm ecstatic about it. I'm sorry if I've hurt you, Janice, but I was pretty cut up myself when you let me take you to bed knowing you'd be emigrating and there was no future for us. Yes, I did like you, an awful lot as it happens, and if you'd stayed here and not gone to live in Australia, I would never have got together with Lisa." I glanced towards the entrance of Lulu's where I saw Jez stood on his own. "Lisa knows about you and she knows how I felt about you but she trusts me. She knows that what we had was very little and it's in the past. I'm not sure what you expect from me, Janice, but what we had has gone and we can never have it back." I'd said my piece, it was time to go back to Jez and get my arse home to bed, though I wasn't building my hopes up about having a good night's sleep.

"So why did you text me, why bother getting in touch with me when your future lay with Lisa?" She had me there.

"I was curious to see how you were getting on. It was a stupid thing to do and Lisa knows about that too."

"Sounds like Lisa has you right where she wants you." She looked over at Jez. "Looks like your friend's waiting. You'd better go."

I tried to smile, hoping we could put all this behind us and move on as friends, but just as I was about to walk away, Janice grabbed me and planted her lips on mine, heavily caressing them for effect, making sure everyone around could see us. It only lasted seconds but I knew that the words she whispered in my ears as she pulled away would stay with me for the rest of my life.

"I love you, Gary Stringer."

She turned on her heels and calmly walked down the stone steps towards the main entrance of Lulu's. I stared after her, not caring that Jez had just witnessed us in a clinch on a public street where absolutely anyone could have seen us, including Lisa.

"You ready, mate?" he said, as I finally found the strength to walk towards him.

"Yeah, take me home."

Chapter Twenty-Four

*J*ez and I stayed up until 4am talking about what could have happened between me and Janice. He promised not to mention that we'd seen her to Lisa though I wasn't sure it was a secret I could keep. I wanted our marriage to start off on the right foot and that didn't involve keeping secrets. I knew she'd be gutted when she heard but it was better coming from me than from a student with a grudge. The problem was, I couldn't tell her before the wedding because she'd made me promise not to contact her, said it was bad luck to see or talk to the bride before the wedding ceremony. Jez had to stop me ringing her a few times but in the end I realised it was for the best. Lisa knew I loved her, she knew how much I wanted to marry her; if she'd have known that I'd been kissed by Janice in Bedworth town centre just hours before I was supposed to make my vows to her, it would have ruined the wedding. In fact, it could even have put a stop to it altogether.

It was a crap night's sleep though Jez's spare bed didn't help with springs prodding in my back and a quilt that was too small. I vowed if I ever stayed at Jez's place again I'd take my own duvet and a blow-up bed. We got up at nine o'clock and Jez made us a full English which went down very nicely. Fortunately, I didn't have a hangover, probably because of all the water and coffee I'd drunk the night before whilst talking to Jez until the early hours. I was dying to ring Lisa, see if she was okay, but Jez insisted I didn't. I switched on my mobile phone to a string of text messages from friends wishing me luck and telling me how lucky I was. I was surprised not to see one from Janice if I'm honest.

We got dressed into our morning suits, Jez looking dapper and handsome with his gold coloured cravat and me looking like a complete tool with my bandy legs. Then Alfie let himself in. The plan was for us all to get dressed at Jez's apartment and go to the church together. It was typical of Alfie to be late but we hadn't heard him come home and usually he made a point of banging his front door and waking up the whole floor of the apartment block.

"You two look like a couple of benders," he laughed.

"Good night, was it?" I asked, taking his suit from the door casing and handing it to him. "You'd better get yourself sorted. We need to leave in an hour."

"I've only just got in. Had a shower, a shave and a shit and thought I'd come and see my two best mates. Cor blimey, Gaz, it was a blinder of a night."

I tutted and rolled my eyes. "I take it you pulled that Alison bird?"

"Pulled her? She nearly fucking killed me. Talk about a goer. I'm seeing her again next weekend."

I thought about Janice. "Where did you go?"

"Back to her place. That Janice bird went home after half an hour, suppose she could see she wasn't wanted. Nice girl but she seemed a bit upset about something. Ali offered to go back with her but she insisted on going by herself."

I turned to Jez. "Maybe I should ring..."

"No," he interrupted, "leave that phone alone, mate."

"But what if she didn't get home last night?" I was starting to worry. Some friend that Alison was.

"Of course she would have got home."

"Have I missed something?" Alfie asked, unzipping the suit bag.

I shook my head slightly, just enough to make Jez see that I didn't want Alfie to know anymore than he did already.

"Nah, nothing, pal. Just this numpty wanting to ring the missus, can't stand being away from her." Jez laughed and walked into the kitchen. "Brew, mate?"

"Coffee, make it strong and black," Alfie replied.

I went into the lounge and sat down, looking at my mobile, wondering if Lisa might have texted me.

"I'd better not look like a ponce," Alfie said, as he walked into the room in just a pair of black boxer shorts.

"You'll look the bee's knees, Alfie. I promise." I put the phone on the coffee table. "How are you anyway, down there like?"

"It's still there, if that's what you mean, my third bollock." We both laughed. "Alison asked me last night if it was okay to touch it."

"Is it, you know, okay, like, does it hurt when you..."

"Shag? Nah, just tingles a bit, but I couldn't feel it last night. That bird's hot. I told her all about it, told her I was having it removed."

"And she still wanted to see you next weekend?" I grinned.

"Yep, I tell you, Gary, she's mad for me. Couldn't get enough of me last night. She wore me out."

I looked at Alfie's rugged complexion, rosy cheeks, bright eyes and huge beaming smile. "Yeah, you look pretty done in to me," I winked.

He left the room and got his suit on, shouting for Jez to help with the cravat. I could hear them laughing and joking in the bedroom, no doubt about the pair of them looking like a couple of bell ends and me being under the thumb, but I didn't care. I loved Lisa. It was her I wanted to spend my life with, I knew that now. It hadn't really needed Janice's outburst last night to confirm that it was Lisa I wanted and not her, but after she'd tried to manipulate me into going to Australia with her, saying I could still see my child, I knew I could never be with her. She'd told me she loved me, something I'd wanted to hear a long time ago, and maybe if I had things would have been so different. But it was too late; she was too late.

❦

People were piling into the church as I sat on the front pew with Jez. I kept turning around to watch Alfie do a fantastic job ushering people to their respective sides of the church. It wasn't a big church but neither of us wanted to get married in a Cathedral. The vicar was standing at the altar reading through some papers, no doubt rehearsing his lecture about marriage being for keeps, whatever happens.

Before I knew it the organ pipes bellowed out 'Here Comes the Bride' and Alfie was standing at the end of the pew telling us Lisa had arrived. My heart jumped into my mouth and my stomach did an Olympic style stomach flip. I was frozen to the spot, unable to turn around and look at my future bride. The music carried on playing while Jez and I stood at the front of the church, the vicar obviously watching Lisa as she glided up the aisle, her arm linked through her dad's. I suspected he was the proudest man alive at that very moment. Jez prodded me in the arm.

"She looks stunning, mate." I hoped he meant Lisa and not Angela, who was her bridesmaid and who I imagined looked equally as gorgeous. And then I did it, I slowly turned my head, craning my neck to see the most beautiful woman I'd ever set eyes on gracefully approach me, dressed in an ivory gown with a veil held in place by a diamond encrusted tiara. I gasped and drew in my breath, almost bowled over by the thought that this woman would soon be my wife.

Lisa stood next to me and smiled. I squeezed her hand and whispered, "You are beautiful." She handed her bouquet to Angela who went to sit down on the front pew next to my mum and Terry. Mum's hat was so wide it almost knocked Angela out and I chuckled to myself as I saw mum's expression trying hard to disguise her annoyance at having to readjust the hat, probably for the hundredth time that day. And then the vicar started the ceremony.

I hated myself for thinking about Janice when he asked, "If anyone knows any reason why these two people should not be joined in matrimony, speak now or forever hold your peace." I didn't dare look around for fear of seeing her behind us with her hand up, ready to ruin our big day. Lisa was confident as she looked at me and smiled, reassuring me that she herself had no reason not to marry me. And then it happened, the church door opened, a latch being lifted followed by the creak of the ancient hinges, followed by the sound of footsteps walking into the building. It was like a horror movie where everyone turns around to face the demon, wondering if this is going to be their last few minutes of existence.

Both Lisa and I turned around at the same time. When I saw Janice standing at the door staring straight at me, the panic rose and I let go of Lisa's hand. What the hell was she playing at? Who the hell did she think she was? Anger was fighting its way out of me and I could see Jez in the corner of my eye shuffling nervously on his feet.

"Shall I have a word?" he whispered to me.

The vicar leant towards me and whispered, "Is everything okay?"

I nodded and turned back to face the altar. If Janice was here to spoil everything I wasn't about to let her. She had no right turning up at my wedding, threatening mine and Lisa's happiness. She could object all she liked but I didn't love her. Lisa was the woman I wanted, not Janice.

"Please carry on," I whispered back, looking at Lisa and smiling.

"Who is she?" Lisa asked me, a little too loudly unfortunately as my mum stood up and came towards us.

"It's Janice," I said.

"I'll tell her to go," mum said. "Did you invite her?"

"Of course I didn't." I was horrified my mum could even think such a thing.

"Then what's she come here for?"

"I don't know. Just tell her to go will you, mum?"

My mum tottered off towards the back of the church where Janice still stood staring at me. I squeezed Lisa's hand and told the vicar to continue.

"Why's she here?" Lisa asked. "How does she know about our wedding?"

"Let's just get married, sweetheart, and I'll fill you in later. Don't let her spoil today."

Lisa withdrew her hand from mine. "Have you been seeing her behind my back?"

"Of course I haven't. I saw her in town last night and told her about the wedding, she tried to talk me out of it but I told her I love you and want to spend the rest of my life with you." I looked at the vicar who was standing looking at me with an expression that could have passed for one of Bethany Calder's brick-shit-house boyfriend's. "Just ignore her, she's a trouble maker."

"I'm going to have a word. No one has any right to come here trying to ruin today. No one!" Lisa turned on her heels and started stomping down the aisle in Janice's direction. My mum was talking quietly to her and she looked mortified as she saw Lisa heading towards her. The whole congregation was now watching the drama unfold, some were whispering among themselves whilst Phillip and Margie were standing up watching their daughter with her virtual sleeves rolled up, going in all guns blazing. I ran after Lisa, Jez on my heels and Alfie following behind.

"What the hell do you think you're doing?" Lisa had no intention of throwing Janice out of the church quietly.

"I wanted to see Gary," Janice began. "What we have is too precious to let go of."

Lisa turned to me. "What you 'have'?" she asked, emphasising the 'have' bit. I cringed.

"We don't have anything," I said, my voice now raised with anger at Janice. "We had this conversation last night. What we 'had' was over a long time ago. You have no right coming here today."

"I love you, Gary," she said, tears streaming down her face.

"You love him?" Lisa screeched, just as her parents arrived at her side. "You buggered off to Australia when you could have had him, but you threw that away. Now you can bugger off home and leave us to get married. How dare you come here trying to steal my groom, how bloody dare you."

Philip put his hand on Lisa's arm. "Calm down, love."

"Don't tell me to calm down, dad. This was supposed to be the most wonderful day of my life, and this..." Lisa threw her arms in the air and looked Janice up and down, "...deranged whore thought she could come here and take my fiancé away." The next thing happened so quickly I think I heard Alfie gasp behind me in horror. Lisa swung her arm around and slapped Janice in the face, and I stared at the great, big red hand mark now painted on Janice's cheek.

"There was no need for that," I said to Lisa, wondering if I would be next.

"Now fuck off and don't ever contact Gary again," Lisa shouted, as the congregation's whispers now materialised into horrified gasps of shock. I don't think the vicar had heard the word 'fuck' said at a wedding ceremony because he sprinted over to us and put his hand on Lisa's arm.

"I think you should take this dispute outside. I'm not comfortable about carrying on the service with you in this state." He was remarkably calm considering a crazed pregnant woman had just walloped her groom's ex-girlfriend in his church.

"We don't need to take anything outside, vicar," Lisa said, turning back toward the altar. "This woman is now leaving and you can carry on with the service." She grabbed my hand. "Gary, we're getting married. Now!"

I learnt that day that it was pointless arguing with Lisa, not that I wanted to of course because I wanted Janice to leave just as much as she did. But the fifty or so guests that made up the congregation all turned around in their seats, bowed their heads and pretended to read the order of service whilst me, Lisa, Jez, Alfie, mum, Philip, Margie and the vicar walked back down the aisle to carry on with our wedding ceremony.

"Our next hymn is 'Lord of All Hopefulness'," the vicar announced as he took his position at the altar.

I'm pleased to say the rest of the wedding went without a hitch. By the time we got outside for the photographs, everyone had calmed down, including Lisa, and it was smiles all round. Even the vicar congratulated us, pointing out it was a bit of touch and go at one point. I imagine it'd be a wedding he'd talk about at the dinner table for a long time to come but he'd done a great job after Janice's ridiculous stunt. Mum hugged me tightly, her hat making a dent in my cheek, whilst Terry shook my hand vigorously, saying "great ceremony, best one I've ever been to."

I had a good look around the church yard to see if Janice was loitering but I couldn't see her. I noticed Lisa looking around at one point and found myself reassuring her that Janice was most probably long gone. My beautiful Lisa, her cleavage now increased due to the pregnancy, just showing enough at the top of her dress, but not enough to look tacky. I had secretly hoped she wouldn't display too much boob as I didn't fancy the thought of all the guys we'd invited eyeing her up, especially when she was carrying our child.

It was gone three o'clock when we finally got a few moments to ourselves. I dragged her into a little side room of the country club where the reception was being held. I pressed my lips hard against hers and caressed her back.

"I can't wait to get you out of this dress," I whispered into her ear, moving my hand around to the front so I could get a good handful of the bodice area.

"I'm sorry I slapped Janice," she said, "but I wasn't going to let her ruin our wedding day." She pulled away slightly. "You're not angry with me for doing that, are you?"

"Of course I'm not, babe. I'm just sorry that I bumped into her last night and told her about our wedding." I thought it better not to mention bumping into her in Marks and Spencer's the other day too.

"I love you so much. We have a wonderful future to look forward to." She kissed me again, her hand now moving towards where my erection was waiting patiently. "Ooh, Gary, does my dress turn you on?"

"No," I replied. "You do."

Suffice to say, our wedding night was pretty damn

incredible. As a surprise, I'd booked the honeymoon suite at the country club, the most expensive room in the hotel, and it was stunning. I helped Lisa out of her dress, my breath blown away when I saw the lingerie she was wearing. I couldn't believe I'd once thought of Lisa as a second choice should Janice not have wanted me. How could I have been so stupid? But as I lay next to Lisa that night, caressing her breasts as she softly breathed against my chest, I knew I was a changed man. My life of philandering and counting up notches on my bedpost was over. And I was now absolutely sure which life I preferred.

The End

Acknowledgements

Special thanks go to my editor, Elaine Denning, for her patience and phenomenal ability not to go insane as she painstakingly edited this book. I suspect she laughed somewhat at my initial use of certain phrases but she tactfully made suggestions that made me realise the importance of not just a good editor, but a great editor. Thanks for sticking with it, Elaine, and for making this book one of my most enjoyable.

A massive thanks once again to Cathy Helms of Avalon Graphics whom I'm sure you will agree, has done a sterling job of the book cover.

Members of Famous Five Plus also deserve a mention for their hard work and support, and for always being there when I've needed advice on grammar, punctuation and which words best suit a sentence. If ever there was a supportive bunch of people in one place, this is the place you'll find them: www.famousfiveplus.com

Thank you to Andrew Brenton of Really Love Your Book who formatted this book for me in both paperback and eBook formats. My technical skills fall way short of attempting this myself and Andrew's assistance has been invaluable.

Another special thanks to Kim Nash, one exceptionally talented lady and good friend who has become my 'beta reader'.

Other Books Available by Kathryn Brown:-

Discovery at Rosehill
Nightingale Woods

Website: www.crystaljigsaw.blogspot.com
Twitter: @CrystalJigsaw

Printed in Great Britain
by Amazon.co.uk, Ltd.,
Marston Gate.